When the Man waked up he said, 'What is Wild Dog doing here?' And the Woman said, 'His name is not Wild Dog any more, but the First Friend, because he will be our friend for always and always and always.

R. Kipling, The Cat that walks by himself.

Now with his master gone he lay there, castaway, on plies of dung from mules and cattle …Infested with ticks, half-dead from neglect, here he lay the hound, old Argos. But the moment he sensed Odysseus standing by he thumped his tail, nuzzling low, and his ears dropped, though he had no strength to drag himself an inch toward his master. Odysseus glanced to the side and flicked away a tear…

Homer, The Odyssey.

We talk of men keeping dogs, but we might often talk more expressively of dogs keeping men.

Charles Dickens, The Uncommercial Traveller.

I

Published by Filament Publishing Ltd
16, Croydon Road, Beddington, Croydon
Surrey CR0 4PA UK
+44 (0)20 8688 2598
www.filamentpublishing.com

An Unwavering Friend by Chris Blazina
ISBN 978-1-913623-62-3

Illustrations by Anne-Marie Sonneveld

Contents

Section III: Healers

Section IV: Adventurers

When man meets dog

*Let me sing to you now about how humans change
into different things.
Ovid, Metamorphoses.*

It seemed fair and perhaps necessary to start the book, a collection of stories about men and dogs, by sharing a little of my own. Canine companions have always been a central part of my life. Scooby was a gentle German Shepherd that guarded the backyard of our family home, but as a boy, he also taught me the gentle art of being a good listener. He sat with me as I shared tales occurring on the other side of the brick wall where ten people were sometimes tensely packed inside a small space. Scooby listened in a very calm and attentive way, the kind of experience that I would later reference in my work as a psychologist. I would think, this is the way to be with people. To put them at ease by listening with genuine care. A dog taught me that skill.

Other dogs entered my life. All rescues. All ones needing a home that in turn, helped me build one for myself. Kelsey, a mixed Golden retriever, was my portable family and friend through graduate school and the beginning of my career. When I lost Kelsey, I felt a palatable thud lasting for years. Being with her taught me many things, including what grief was - it is the flip side of love. In her memory, I began a new part of my professional focus, trying to figure out why dogs mean so much to us. Especially why men need them. Research studies, articles, and books became venues to understand more about the power of our bond, how it changes our lives, or at the very least makes the difficulties we experience more manageable. I learned things that became evident in my practice but also in my own life - dogs help many of us become better social creatures. They teach us what it means to form and sustain important relationships. The hard work that it entails, and how it can lead to profoundly caring connections. The result is something psychoanalyst Sigmund Freud referred to as pure love - a deep affection our dogs provide for us that lacks the normal ambivalent feelings that shows up in most all other relationships. It means they gladly give their full self to us. In turn, we learn from that bond, and in our better moments, our better selves appear.

Studies over the years also pointed out the challenges men experience with their dogs. I believe it is true that our ties make many of us better at real relationships. However, as we age, so many middle-aged men see their support networks shrink to the size of a postage stamp. Usually, a romantic partner and a dog. But dogs do not live forever. That is when pure love turns to pure grief. It is also when most of us lose at least half of our network of social support. Making matters even worse, most men have been taught to conceal tender feelings that even apply to the connection and loss of our beloved canine friends. One of the most telling studies was men trying to hide or under-report to others how important their dogs are to them. Due in large part to the concern of not being understood. In all these findings, I see a part of my own experience.

Sadie was without doubt the best friend of my life. A Border Collie with an undying loyalty and devotion that graced my life for more than 16 years. I can still remember the last six months of her life, sitting under the stars together when her discomfort made it too difficult to sleep. I recall our last walk before saying goodbye. How she was a fighter to the very end. The dream that I had after she passed, where she transformed from a dog howling at night to a majestic white wolf making her way through the forest. It told me she was going to be alright. Maybe, me as well.

Sadie sat with me as I began writing this book. That familiar place under my desk. After she passed, I thought of tangible ways to remember our friendship. I keep a little statue of her near my writing area. Her memory is reflected in the form of an inked dog paw with the accompanying Latin phrase underneath - "Neque Seorsum- "Never Parted." This remembrance rests peacefully on my left arm.

Other dogs are still with me in the present day. Beatrix, Marley, Tex, and Dusty. A mix of Border Collies and Goldens. Each shaping my life and offering inspiration. Friends with four paws. A collection of unwavering companions.

After studying the lives of men who appear in this book, I concluded I was part of a community that I did not know existed. Dickens, Darwin, Byrd, and Freud. All friends that I never knew but nonetheless feel connected to through their love of dogs. It struck me one day that I took a cue from these men. To really understand who they were you must look to their dogs. The bond reveals an aspect of men that was not commonly known or in some cases, purposefully hidden from view. To really see these places where man meets dog offers a fresh perspective, windows into the best parts of who we are.

I think back 50 years ago to when I was 5 years-old. At the time I was somewhat obsessed with drawing dogs driving cars. Recently, I unfolded one of these masterpieces that I had tucked away long ago. On the back of the image was my child-like scrawl explaining the drawing on the other side. The words referred to the canine in the driver's seat. But what caught my attention was the mention of "Chris Dog" a reference to my own pedigree. By my reckoning, I was part dog. The piece itself was not exactly a foreshadowing of a promising art career. Instead, it spoke to the way I would motor through my life, with a canine companion at my side.

Introduction

Recently, I read an article claiming, 'Men who have dogs make the best husbands.' I scanned through the explanation and some of the purported characteristics these gentlemen were supposed to possess. The writer argued dog-owning men were loyal and considerate, or at least had some capacity to think beyond themselves. Also, it was suggested that males who have dogs were not afraid of commitment; anyone that has ever had an animal companion can attest to the need for daily investment of time and energy for things to be right. Lastly, there was the assertion the man-dog bond helps men learn how to be emotionally expressive and are in fact better partners and parents. The commentary left me thinking dogs are rightfully considered man's best friend. Canine companions help many of us become better skilled at relationships or at least provide one connection in the often socially isolated world of being a man.

To be honest, I am not sure all the men found in this book were good husband or even friend material. In fact, history tells us some are known to be just the opposite. However, I feel more assured that even the most hardened, emotionally detached males are usually better off for having an animal companion. We are elevated to a different level of existence by having a dog in our midst. Some males just have further ways to go in our emotional development. Each chapter in this book offers readers a glimpse into pivotal instances when a dog impacted a man's life. At times, these are brief encounters lasting just a few moments, for others, it is the stuff literally of legend where the very nature of a man is not only challenged but changed through the sustained contact with an animal companion.

When researching and writing the stories of men and dogs, I found that in several cases there was less than six degrees of separation between the people I discuss. In some instances, one man's story leads directly to another. I wondered about how this overlap occurred? Was it men who bonded with dogs were drawn together by a stroke of luck or the social circles that they frequented? Or is it that men had been deeply affected by the connection with man's best friend somehow could recognize the quality in one another? Perhaps it is an understated and unspoken gesture which signals membership in this less well-known fraternal order - the brotherhood of the bond. Within its ranks are artists, creative thinkers, adventurers, healers, and underdogs. By no means is this an exhaustive list of categories nor are all members present and accounted for in the chapters that follow. One might even argue some of these men belong to more than one grouping in the society.

At the end of the day, this book is a sampling of stories. Ones that I hope provide some insight into the nature of how men are affected by dogs. Charter members over the past two hundred years include Charles Dickens, Charles Darwin, and Sigmund Freud. When I began assembling the facts for each story, my own curiosity was piqued about each person and dog. Of course, some of these tales could stand on their merit just by chronicling the details. But I also wanted to convey a three-dimensional picture of each man whenever possible. Depending upon the available source material there are varying degrees of complexity that can be offered on what made each man tick. In many ways, I approached each man's story in the way that I do in my work as a psychologist – my curiosity about how the pieces of a person's life fit together. The result is I can speculate about another topic, how a dog touched each man's life in a significant way.

Nearly all stories in the book concern actual historical figures. However, in one instance the man in question is clearly from the mythical realm. Odysseus, the hero in Homer's Epic the Odyssey is the rare exception. His entry into the brotherhood is derived from being considered the "first modern man." The status is bestowed in large part due to his personal complexity. He moves far beyond the simple good guy versus bad guy status still seen in many of today's storylines. Instead, he is multifaceted and clearly imperfect. But it is his flawed nature that makes him relatable. When we read about Odysseus we might resonate with his struggles or style of approaching scenarios. Initially that may be startling or even disconcerting. Ultimately, though, I found it not only revealing but also comforting. Today, many of our own personal stories (mine included) pale by comparison in terms of scale and importance to those that are mentioned in this book. However, it is the common theme that unites all members of the brotherhood. These places of connection tell us we are not alone. Case in point, constructing each man's backstory also led to this unforeseen benefit - I felt like I got to know many of these men. Even though all of them have long since departed, some I now consider a friend. Dogs draw us together in sometimes unanticipated ways.

At the heart of things, the bond with dogs speaks to a fundamental need we all have in forming and sustaining a connection with another: one of the quintessential psychological needs we all have as social creatures. This need for bonding is true for everyone even if some of us have not fully realized the sentiment applies to us. For instance, males often keep to ourselves, and force others of the two-legged variety, even those that we care about, to piece together the goings-on of our inner world. It leaves many guessing in regards to who we are, what we feel and need. In the worst case, when others sense our distance, we just seem impossibly stubborn and forlorn giving the impression not only do we not want the company of others, we also do not need it. These various missteps do a fine job of keeping others away. They also give many the wrong impressions about a deeper, more hidden part of our nature we often do not allow others to see.

The well-worn scenario of a loner that does not report feeling alone may be an apt description for how many men are among their human companions. But the description does not fit when interacting with our dogs. Men let our guards down in a dog's presence. We relax and comfortably abide within our connection. Dogs see us at our worst. Sometimes they even witness a few precious moments when we rise above ourselves, perhaps become the kind of men they hoped us to be. Maybe the easiness we share with our dogs is the result of spending more than 10,000 years in each other's company. I sometimes imagine the context has changed over the millennia but some of the problems have not. Even men from antiquity probably bemoaned their work conditions and seemingly clueless bosses. The same collective also probably sought guidance concerning our unintended slip-ups with family and friends. All the while our dogs accompany us on walks in the wilderness, watching and listening with seeming interest as we recount the most recent troubles from our personal narrative. A task they have already done numerous times before. Ultimately, the bond supplies the means to be more whole men. We can flip the switch on a part of ourselves that has been waiting to be shared for some time. Canine companions attend us in unfettered ways as we journey into our most private moments of thinking and feeling. If we are truly fortunate, what we learn from the bond sets a foundation to be a successful social creature in other circumstances, allowing us to be better partners, parents, and friends.

This book explores the unique bond between men and dogs. However, it is important to say that the bond with animal companions is not something that belongs exclusively to the world of males, nor are dogs the only type of companion that can touch us so deeply. I have chosen to write about men and dogs because it is a story I know personally. As in the case of Rudyard Kipling's story, a dog was the "first friend" that made so much else possible. Likewise, the title of one chapter, "I dream of that dog yet" is a quote taken from dogsled legend Arthur Walden when reminiscing about the passing of his companion Chinook. Sometimes the bond's full measure is not understood at the time we are together sharing adventures of various kinds but only fully revealed after losing our special friend. Yet, the memory of our animal companions is not something we go back to time again to just piece together the mystery of how things came to be. Instead, these warm recollections sustain many of us in the darkest moments as well as being a central part of the brightest days.

There is a universal quality to the bond with animal companions that has a deep appeal for all. That is, if we can open ourselves to the experience of a non-human animal that differs from us in the words of Charles Darwin "in degree rather than kind." We have a bond with a dog. 'Bond' being the operative code word for a relationship that feels like a close friend or family member. What makes this possible? Some have suggested the bond is appealing because it consists of the best human characteristics such as warmth and acceptance. That is a good place to start but we must look closer. When we stare deeply into the much-lauded hearts of dogs we see a union of opposites; a condition that might be judged in more human circumstances as a living contradiction of terms. There is a prevailing simplicity in dogs' interactions that are anything but 'simple'. Sigmund Freud once remarked about the un-ambivalent nature of dogs. They love their friends and bite their enemies. You always know where you stand with them. There is no guesswork or deciphering of unclear gestures as in the case of so many of our human relations. That type of connection offers many of us a visceral sense of safety. No surprises. No betrayals. Just a chance to experience pure love, a condition that solidifies forever after twelve to fourteen years of being in each other's company.

In more complex terms a dog's simple attributes do much to right the ship when the sum total of our human relations seems marred by disappointment and frustration. When too much of our lives are strained by these aforementioned conditions most of us are familiar with the need to pull back into a safer and more well-defended space. In more than a few cases this is when a special dog shows up making a life-altering appearance. The same sequence of events is relevant for many of the men in this book. Though it would not be accurate to assume that the bond only appeals to us in those moments when we are at our most vulnerable. Instead, animal companions add to our existence in various stages of our lives, and under many easy and difficult circumstances.

I have two photos of men and dogs in the office where I do most of my writing. One is of an elderly and frail looking Sigmund Freud seated with his Chow Luna. Luna is standing on her back legs having placed her front paws onto Freud's lap as if the two are about to embrace. Freud looks intensely at Luna with a mixed expression of tenderness and sadness. He seems so caught in the moment Freud is either unaware or unconcerned by someone taking such an intimate photograph. This struck me because Freud was known to be over-controlling with so many aspects of his life including new science psychoanalysis. But this photo captures a moment when Freud let his vulnerability show. It seems fitting as we will see later that it should be with a dog.

The other photo is of the 20th century's "last explorer" Admiral Richard E. Byrd and his dog Igloo. The locale is the bottom of the world with glaciers and snow acting as a polar backdrop. The little terrier is on his hind legs doing a version of a hug, his front legs wrapped around Byrd's, the dog's head not quite reaching the man's waist. Byrd places his arm around Igloo as they both peer into the camera.

Even in the frozen world of Antarctica, the coldest place on the planet, the dynamic duo seems to be pausing just for one moment before leaping into action, exploring the undiscovered country.

Both photos provided inspiration when working on this book, both being explorers, one of the inner worlds and the other its counterpart in the external one. However, as I uncovered one story after another concerning men and dogs, I realized if the standard for joining Freud and Byrd was some form of a heart-felt tale, I could decorate all four walls of my office with similar photographs and illustrations. I was surprised at the depth and touching nature of these men's narratives. Even cynical and broken men held tenderness for their canine companions.

Some of the stories of men and dogs are moving and others are humorous. A few pull for a deep level of pathos, even when involving men that have personal qualities that may be judged as less than sympathetic. However, all the stories illustrate the unique bond with man's best friend. Men across history have found canine friends a source of companionship. The book is as much about extraordinary animals as the men who were befriended by them.

Section I: Artists & Thinkers

Historians and archaeologists tell us that there are stories concerning mankind's bond with dogs dating back to ancient Egypt. These tales include the burial rituals that offered owners assurance they would reunite with their dogs in the afterlife. While we might expect that to occur among Egypt's ruling elite that includes queens and pharaohs, there are also instances like the everyman Hapi-men who was buried with a small dog at his feet.

We can go back further in time to the occurrence at the Chauvet Cave in France. Here archeologists discovered the footprints of a human boy about eight years-old who by their estimates stood four-and-a-half feet tall. His prints indicate he was walking in the cave around the area known as the room of skulls believed to carry ceremonial significance. At some point he slipped and then stopped to clean his torch. Paw prints of a large canid with a shortened middle digit on the front paw - a characteristic of dogs - were also found in proximity to the boy. The position of the boy's and dog's tracks have led some to conclude the jaunt into the Chauvet Cave was a joint expedition. If that is correct, that would be one of oldest evidence to date of the shared bond with dogs dating back between 20,000-30,000 years. Those prints are literally etched in history.

While there is much to be said for stories from antiquity, most of the ones found in this book are taken from the past two centuries. When I was researching man and dog stories my attention kept getting drawn back to this timeframe. Even much older tales are often recycled here, a period I will refer to as the 'Age of the Dog.' With the advent of this new companion animal age, this does not mean that man and dog were not friends long before this time, nor does it mean that the cruelty or neglect dogs sometimes experienced at the hand's society and occasionally by their owners was all but eradicated. It just implies that what we know today as our version of man's best friend began taking shape here in familiar and powerful ways.

During the Age of Dog humanity, especially in Western locales, began taking a different notice of Canis familiaris. There are at least two theories about how this transformation occurred. One involves a scarcity of human-animal interaction, especially by urban dwellers. To make up for this vacuum it is suggested humans developed a more widespread connection with our domesticated friends. The other notion suggests it was not so much a dearth of contact that changed our point of view (at least not at first) but rather it is the quality of human-animal interaction that alters our point of view. The result is the development of a more dog friendly perspective. I am inclined to say there is some merit in both theories blended together.

Two Theories on the Age of Dog

In 1815 London was already the largest city in the world. But the city would incur a population explosion over the next one hundred years. By 1860 it had tripled to reach over 3 million inhabitants, and then doubled again to include a population of over seven million by 1910. As London grew, new sanitation regulations were imposed. One of the results was that animals that were commonplace began disappearing from the streets. Subsequently, the previous practice of farmers and drovers regularly herding cattle and sheep through the center of town also changed. This way of doing business began disappearing by the mid-19th century or some argue as late as by the turn of the 20th century. It was as if something symbolic was occurring, removing a certain natural element that might not fit with the new order of things. Some argue that the Western world became increasingly separated from the agrarian way of life and with it, animals that were rooted in our psyches so many millennia ago.

These changes to our relationship with the natural world were all a part of the progress associated with the Industrial Age. The movement is responsible for modernizing the world for a bigger and better lifestyle. Yes, it is good to have electric lights, travelable roads, and easier access to harvested crops. But modernity did not always consider how certain key elements were also left behind. Elements many believe our collective health and well-being were founded upon.

However, a person did not have to live in the world's biggest city to feel modernity's effects. In a similar way, the United States also began experiencing the impact of the Industrial age and with it, changes to the relationship with man's best friend.

As Mark Derr notes in A Dog's History of America, the dog became an intermediary for humans among the many cultural changes and conflicts not limited to town versus country and civilized versus wild. As we changed, so did dogs, they adapted to our needs. A working dog on America's frontier was essential for the survival for those hunters and pioneers trying to live in the wilderness. Today, working dogs have a different job description. Many tend to our emotional needs for companionship amid a different kind of societal isolation. They have adapted yet again to the changing modern landscape of humanity.

The first theory that humans of the 19th & 20th centuries found themselves particularly drawn to natural surroundings was an attempt to counterbalance the Industrial Age's change of venue. Replacing rolling green hills with rolls of tenement buildings left something to be desired. Turning back the clock a few hundred years to the beginning of the Age of Dog and we see various movements trying to counterbalance the Industrial Age's growing hold. There are European Romantic era writers and then the American Transcendentalists, both of whom called for a return to a relationship with the natural world. There was a worry about an ever-increasing mechanized world that left nature out of the equation.

The second theory of how the Age of Dog came to be is as the result of an array of changes occurring with our relationship with animals especially in the 19th century. Much of this happens in the form of entertainment for the masses and then also through the scientific studies of animals and then later, that of the psychology of human-animal interaction. When we re-examine our relationship with animals through new optics, long standing beliefs begin to transform. For example, animals, especially dogs became the subject of well-loved Victorian painters like Edwin Landseer and Briton Reverie. Many of these paintings attributed sentimental and human-like quality to canines in a variety of scenarios. Dogs were depicted as grieving deeply for their lost masters. They also played in rousing fashion with each other and humans across the life span from the very young to the very old. Dogs were even portrayed as possessing child-like qualities that were not limited to a purity of heart. Cute, mischievous, and heart stealing canines also stole the scenes in many of these painted depictions of Victorian life. While the original artworks hung in the homes of wealthy patrons, the work of engravers allowed copies to be distributed within the middle class. With the advent of advertising in the early 20th century, even those from the working class could have access to cheaply reproduced copies. The latter was accomplished as a marketing tool where products like a bar of soap was parried with a reproduction of a painting illustrating the fidelity of a dog. Both would never let customers down, that is, if they possessed the required number of proofs of purchase coupons to complete the exchange for their copy of the work of art.

The Greatest Show on Earth

The advent of the modern-day circus is also responsible for bringing the greatest show on earth to town. Philip Astley opened the first modern circus in 1768 in England. In these early circuses' patrons witnessed mostly demonstrations of equestrian expertise. Not to be outdone, John Bill Ricketts brought the first circus to the United States in 1792. Over the next fifty years, master of ceremonies P. T. Barnum added three rings of entertainment and circus trains to transport the show between locales. In the earliest forms of circus, most animals were viewed in menageries, that is, enclosed spaces that patrons could safely view from a distance. Perhaps for a few moments spectators felt like they had contact with something wild.

Modern zoos took the menagerie to a new level of public and permanent exhibition. Zoos could also be viewed as more than merely representing entertainment value, instead they took on a new scientific meaning in the 18th century's Age of Enlightenment. Here science, reason, and logic were upheld as the new cultural ideals ushering the populace from the darker ages of long held beliefs and superstitions. The same principles of the age extended to the study of non-human animals in the 19th century – zoology. The first modern zoo opened in Paris, France in 1793. The London Zoo was not far behind in April 1828.

In 1838, just a year and half after returning from his voyage on the HMS Beagle, naturalist Charles Darwin visited the London Zoo in order to make the acquaintance of Jenny the orangutan. Jenny was the first ape Darwin ever encountered, although in this case she was adorned in a dress to amuse zoo visitors. Darwin climbed into the cage alone with Jenny. On this and two other subsequent visits, he did simple experiments like holding up a mirror and making note of her emotional expressions, as the zookeeper teased her with the promise of an apple for good behavior. Darwin notes, Jenny was "astonished beyond measure" when she saw her reflection. Jenny made a profound impression on Darwin. Some believed this was another step toward solidifying his theory of evolution.

Zoos gave humans the opportunity to see an intriguing reflection of their own animal nature although a visitor may not grasp its full significance or meaning. In fact, some might witness behavior unbecoming of civilized human beings and conclude Mr. Darwin's assertions about man and ape sharing the same ancestor were anything but creditable. It may have given others a sense of power and importance that a caged animal with incredible prowess and intelligence could be examined in the same way as a selection from one's stamp collection. But for some, seeing Jenny and the other animals that followed involved more than a Sunday outing to see exotic 'beasts' from a distant land. Instead, they saw a caged animal that longed to be free and somehow these visitors understood why.

Harriet Ritvo in the book Animal Estate also pondered the question of Victorian England's growing fascination with animals. Ritvo suggests a similar way of tracing our relationship with animals through the growing popularity of zoology books. Readers enjoyed thumbing through pictorial depictions of animals that were located both near and far away. But most of the pages in such books were allotted to the animals seen as closest to humanity. Those that were willingly domesticated and serving mankind. By doing so those animals elevating their own status. While a horse fulfilled various necessary roles for the country gentleman as well as the city dweller, it was the dog that received most praise. It had to do with their noble nature and the undying sense of loyalty.

Dogs were even willing to submit to the punishment for misdeeds all the while as Ritvo observes, licking their master's hand. We might argue that besides trying to preserve a sense that humans are incontrovertibly alone at the top of the human-animal web, something else was also at work. The result was questioning the human-animal status quo. Until then, the hierarchy that had been long since established, placed mankind as the sole proprietor of the natural world. All of nature's bounty - flora, fauna, and animals existing exclusively for human being's picking. What was left out of this narrow point of view was not only the welfare of animals but how nature's presence impacted humans for the better.

The Pet Effect

In the latter part of the twenty century there came the advent of the scientific study of nature's positive influence on both human's physical and mental well-being. From E.O. Wilson's perspective the need to connect with nature is something deeply embedded within our psyches. He suggests the term biophilia, "the urge to affiliate with other forms of life." Further, the investigation of nature's impact is broadly referred to as ecopsychology. From an ecopsychology perspective, a setting, especially our home that incorporates elements of the natural world, sets the foundation for the beginnings of healthy living and even possibly becoming a healing sanctuary. We even try to augment our urban surroundings adding organic elements. Such nature inspired décor and design elements include pictures of landscapes or even a fish tank filled with fins and flora. Or it could involve windows that allow for natural light and give us access to views of the landscape. On a community level, urbanites incorporate green spaces, so for a few moments, we transcend the concrete jungle and our regularly disconnected surroundings.

If nature is a remedy for modern ills, there is still a concern about how to find a regular communion with it. Perhaps if we are separated from it, we turn our minds to find new ways of bringing it nearer, especially for those not fortunate enough to dwell within an ecopsychology certified home. While Eco vacations or the mass migration to national parks might be ways of capturing a special one-time outing, it is the dog that we rely upon for a natural encounter on a daily basis. Having a dog in our midst teaches us something of how to straddle the domestic world of home with that of the wild woods that lie just beyond our backyards. Psychologist Boris Levinson argued in the 1960's that many of the modern troubles of society are due to a long-standing disconnect from elements of the natural world. Levinson suggested that a reconnection with nature could be reestablished through good relationships with animal companions. Dogs become the "halfway station" on the road back to human completeness. The positive results are sometimes referred to as the pet effect.

The stories in this section of the book illustrate our changing relationship with canine companions in the Age of Dog. These artists & thinkers made note of these changes in different lived ways, each holding a piece of the puzzle.

Only by assembling the various parts does the newly revised image come into view.

If we can call to mind the day some twenty thousand years ago, when a small boy and dog entered the Chauvet Cave, we might prepare ourselves for an everyday encounter that actually borders on the mythological. We are transported by our bond with dogs to a special realm. The inquisitive nature of one party on two legs and the other on four leaving tracks for those that will one day follow behind...

Section I: Artists & Thinkers

Home

"We talk of men keeping dogs, but we might often talk more expressively of dogs keeping men"

Charles Dickens, The Uncommercial Traveller

19th century London was a city of extremes. There were those of wealth and privilege, and then those that only knew extreme poverty. For the millions that fell into the latter category, many lived in overcrowded and unsanitary slums. The four walls of these 'homes' carried with them dangers both inside and out making inhabitants susceptible to illness and death. Tenement houses were commonly built upon cheap land that could be rented as multifamily dwellings. In some cases, housing had less than a firm and healthy foundation that included being built over cesspools. The overall poor sanitation conditions for most of London lead to outbreaks of typhoid and dysentery. At its worst, the infant and child mortality rates were staggering, half the children died before reaching their fifth birthday. If they did survive till age ten, children joined the full-time work force alongside adults. Among the poor, the workdays were long and dangerous - a 16-hour day, six to seven days a week of work was common. At the time of Dickens' birth in 1812, the average adult Londoner born into the professional class had a life expectancy of 27 years. For the poor, it was just 22 years.

Within months of Dickens's death in 1871 biographies began appearing and still are being published up to the current day. Some of the earliest written were by close friends or family members, offering the public new details on an already carefully honed public image. Those that came later do not focus on Dickens as a saint but rather as a very human being. To understand how dogs fit into his life means appreciating Charles Dickens as a private, complex, and sometimes troubled man.

In his many books, Dickens immortalized the stark realities of life on London's mean streets and the difficult lives of the poor. Within these desperate conditions, it may seem far fetched to speak of the comforts of home. In one of Dickens' novels, "Bleak House," Jo the sweeper literally does not know what the word "Home" means. But even amid these difficulties Dickens offers his characters and subsequently his readers, a hope that things could be better. Each search to find a safe haven. Home on one level involves finding a physical location that is warm, well-lit, and provides shelter. However, above all else, home is a state-of-mind, a place where you belong. It consists of a family either joined by blood, or circumstances, where someone cares. We need to appreciate something of Dickens's own life to understand how he held a similar preoccupation as the characters he created. But if one were to study the life of Dickens it could be easily said his story reads like one of his novels.

Dickens' ability to capture the plight of the poor is borne from his unique ability to observe others committing experiences from both childhood and adult circumstances to memory becoming the stuff of his literary creations. The keen powers of observation also have something to do with writing his own personal story, albeit in disguised form. At the age of twelve Charles began the role of sole breadwinner for himself (and his family) through employment in a rat-infested boot blackening shop. At the time, his parents were serving two years in debtors' prison. Debtors' prison is a far cry from today's bankruptcy law and involved instead a court-ordered judgment to work off debt through hard labor or until you were lucky enough to have someone with funds to bail you out. Subsequently Dickens knew firsthand what it meant to feel like a stray, left to the mercy of unfriendly surroundings. His family was eventually able to pay off their debt only through the death of a wealthy relative. Michael Slater chronicles in Dickens and Women that Charles' first of many dysfunctional connections' women started with his mother. After the family's situation improved, she made the thirteen-year-old Charles return to the dye shop in order to help shore up the family's finances. Dickens never forgave or forgot that sequence of events.

Fred Kaplan writes in his biography titled Dickens: *A Biography*, that all the abandoned and neglected children in Dickens's fictional works were central to his own identity. The child characters tell stories that resonated with a portion of Dickens' own experience. Others note that Dickens never really worked through the childhood despair that characterized his formative years. Dickens makes note of the hardship and his inability to understand why things occurred as they did:

> … I could have been so easily cast away at such an age…. No advice, no counsel, no encouragement, no consolation, no support, from any one that I can call to mind, so help me God.

It is very important to recognize Dickens' sense of painful loneliness as a child and a strong desire to escape the financial and emotional circumstances that had a hold of his family. These themes were core to who Dickens the man would later become. The day his father was taken away to debtor's prison he told young Charles the sun had now set on his life and what is also implied with it, so had his son's. Or at the very least, Charles was truly on his own. Dickens' own money management skills and drive to succeed seemed to surpass his father's even at the age 12 years of age. Dickens took his pay from the shoe blackening position and wrapped the daily allotment of expenses in individual pieces of paper marked for each day of the week. The precaution was taken to prevent overspending.

Dickens' fear of never having enough would follow him throughout his life, a source of his tremendous work ethic. He would not follow in his father's footsteps at any cost.

Dickens writes later as an adult about these childhood recollections with a pathos that mirrors any of the sad circumstances of his novel's characters. While he could be very charming and playful, he saw himself as an outsider, a boy and later man that saw much and felt very deeply about it. It included a sense of shame and strict privacy about the circumstances of his upbringing. His grandparents were servants. His father avoided the same circumstances by the good fortune of a family friend. The senior Dickens was given a chance to have a bit more working for the navy pay office but was always pressed for funds. The background and the hard times that would ensue colored life for Dickens. As a young man, Dickens felt self-conscious and unfamiliar with the appropriate social nuances encountered in more refined circles. His first love jilted him due to poor prospects. Those events would only be revealed as an adult to his best friend John Forster, who only after Dickens death revealed some aspects in the biography he wrote.

There is a sense of a type of emotional pressure cooker in Dickens' life. Some tension regarding formative life circumstances was likely both stoked and relieved on his daily walks through the doggy side of London. He framed his long walks, sometimes as much as twenty miles a day, as doing research for his novels and taking a much-needed daily constitutional. But it also seemed to be a revisiting of his own thoughts and feelings. Those that so shaped him and continued to haunt as well as inspire him.

What is also noteworthy is Dickens would become involved time and again with those in tragic or dire circumstances willing to help in any way he could. This might be a chance encounter on the streets, or later, when he helped establish a school for the poor and a type of safehouse for women that had no choice but to take on the world's oldest profession. One could easily conclude that Dickens saw himself in these various circumstances and wanted to help.

One lesser appreciated aspect of Dickens' work was how he utilized animals in his novels. He would characterize a person by how he or she treated them. In other instances, he alluded to a shared forlorn disposition of both the street dwelling humans and dogs. Both of whom longing to find a friend and within whose companionship afforded a type of home. In this version of home, an actual permanent physical communal space may be less likely that a state of mind temporally shared between two outsiders.

Dickens' use of dogs was not just a literary technique. He had a special connection with animals. He studied them like he did people, these observations providing the backstory for many of his characters. He kept many types of animals at his home that included horses, birds, cats, but it was dogs that held the most special place. In fact, his daughter Mamie commented after Dickens' death, "I think his strongest love, among animals, was for dogs."

As a youth, Dickens wrote a letter to an associate that identified himself as a type of lost dog, one whose collar bore the initials "CD" upon it. As an adult after finding literary fame, Dickens surrounded himself with dogs at Gad's Hill Place, his country home in Kent, England. He even kept statutes of canines on his writing desk and carried little dog figurines in his coat pocket. What can be surmised is that animal companions not only provided a distraction from or inspiration for his work, but they also helped raise his spirits. While Dickens temperament was mercurial, fully engaging one moment and cool and aloof the next, it was during especially difficult times his bond with dogs seemed present.

Dickens' life was especially turbulent in his middle years. He was estranged from his wife Catherine with whom he had ten children. There were unkindnesses toward Catherine in both public and private realms. He wrote to his closest friends of their incompatibly. Public statements in newspapers were also made by Dickens attesting to the same! He also tried to keep his other romantic matters with his much younger mistress (Nelly Ternan) from public view. Ternan was nearly thirty years his junior. In one instance these various efforts collided in an unseemly way. Jewelry intended for his mistress was mistakenly delivered to Catherine. Dickens made her deliver the necklace to Nelly in person, driving home the point that the marriage was over. Again, confidant John Forster comments on Dickens' struggles saying, he is a good man, trying to be a good man in a difficult situation. Perhaps most revealing into Dickens' psyche comes from a visit he had in 1862 with Russian writer Dostoevsky. He was an admirer of Dickens and took comfort from *David Copperfield* when he was feeling down. Charles Dickens reveals to him that all his characters are at least in part a reflection of his own persona. The good ones reflecting more aspirational heroic qualities, while the villainous ones his darker nature. Given this insight occurred only eight years before his death, we can see Charles is sorting through his life and subsequent struggles.

It may come as no surprise, Dickens' novels also took a turn toward the darker side during this period such as *Bleak House*, a commentary of British society's hypocrisy related to class issues. Dickens' daughter Katy offered a view into the climate of the Dickens household at this time: "Nothing could surpass the misery and unhappiness of our home."

To be fair, Dickens already had an established tie with specific dogs but amid these hard times, Dickens found a new appreciation for the bond with canine companions. Even long before he owned a dog, Dickens' first published story in 1833, "A Dinner At Poplar Walk," in London's The Monthly Magazine, contains one. The dog appears as an unruly guest in the home of an uptight bachelor gnawing curtains and trying to steal food from the man's table.

Dickens' first dog was called Timber, a white Havanese spaniel that was a gift from a friend. Dickens was 30 years old. He taught Timber a few tricks like jumping over a stick and standing on two legs. An impressive accomplishment for a breed standing only 8–11 inches at the shoulder. Over their almost twelve years together (1843 to 1854), Timber is frequently mentioned in many of Dickens's letters, some note, more so than his wife Catherine. He writes amusing anecdotes about Timber ranging from an unfortunate fall from a carriage, to the dog becoming incensed by being infested with fleas.

Almost all of Dickens' later dogs were large breeds - Bloodhounds, St Bernards, Newfoundlands, and dogs of unknown origins. None of whom were taught tricks as in the case of Timber. Instead, Dickens walked with his dogs, and they assumed the role of guardian for his family. Turk was a mastiff-type breed Dickens had for eight years. In one episode

Dickens mistakes a swollen and likely gouty foot for a minor case of frostbite. He still puts on his boots and wanders with difficulty through the snow in the woods that surrounds his Gad'sHouse country home. Upon his return journey of three miles, he becomes fully lame. There is perhaps a momentary remembering of what it was like to be frightened and on his own as a child. To his surprise, Dickens suddenly beholds two large dogs staring at him through the woods. He realizes both are his and one is Turk. Dickens recalls how he felt as each dog stayed in step with him for the entire journey home, never once moving ahead or away from him.

A surface examination of this story may be simply taken as another one of Dickens' lively anecdotes constructed for the entertainment of his readers. However, if viewed in deeper terms, the story is revealing in the context of Dickens' own life. The boy and later man who often felt on his own, has a markedly different experience with his dogs. One that encapsulates his hoped-for fantasy of having a reliable relation that would be there for him in his moments of distress. His dogs see his vulnerability and do not desert him. Instead, they walk stride for stride along with Dickens never leaving him behind. This is such a contrast to his relationship with his father and mother who Dickens felt abandoned by. Many others in his adult years seemed to evoke a similar level of disappointment. This included publishers that did not share his enthusiasm for book ideas, including A Christmas Carol that was rejected by his usual publisher (Chapman & Hill) and was instead, self-published. Or friends and other family relations that fell by the wayside for making the unforgivable mistake of not staying loyal or steady (at least in his eyes). This even a occurred with his closest and lifelong friend John Forster who might be described with some of the same nomenclature of a dog equivalent - loyal and friendly – but nonetheless there were periods of tension and estrangement, mostly at Dickens doing. Dickens anger would often appear in moments of frustration and despondency, withdrawing and cutting people off. Within the context of human relations, his dogs did something so many others could not. Upon Turks' untimely death, due to a railroad accident, it was said that Dickens grieved deeply. What he lost in Turk's passing is both real and symbolic. A friendship that fulfils the basic emotional needs that so many dog owners know about – an unwavering friend.

Some of Dickens' large dogs fared better than others. A young admirer named Percy Fitzgerald wrote an article about Dickens comparing him to the Victorian Painter Edwin Landseer. Percy argues both artists are to be credited for Parliament's adoption of new humane laws for dogs. But if one were forced to choose between the two, Dickens is the greater by virtue of being a painter of words. Dickens was flattered and began visits with his new friend. Talks were pleasant and included the topic of dogs. Percy gave Dickens Sultan in 1865 about a month after Turk's death.

Sultan was a large dog of uncertain breed, a Spanish mastiff, and/or Irish bloodhound mix. He was ferocious and meant at first to be the protector of the interior of the Dickens home, but he bit his way through doors. After which, it was thought best to keep him chained and muzzled in the front yard. While what occurred next is a matter of some debate, and possibly some revision of history on behalf of his daughter who told the tale at different times in different ways, what was certain was that Sultan bit a child badly. The next day Dickens has one of the servants put Sultan down with a single shot of a gun. He writes about the events in letters to friends over the next four months. The pathos is evident for the dog and child in these accounts but Dickens, some claim, is emotionally removed in the writing. However, in Beryl Grays' The Dog in the Dickensian Imagination, she claims Dickens uses a 'comic serious' manner of dealing with Sultan's fate. This type of blunted approach to loss would have been understandable for someone like Dickens that knew about loss firsthand, but had difficulty grieving openly. Gray concludes even if Dickens did not always make the best decisions for his dogs this did not keep him from being deeply affected by their suffering.

A notable exception to the large size rule was his daughter Mamie's dog Mrs. Bouncer, a Pomeranian. Dickens gifted the dog to his daughter in 1859. Mamie later recalls that in the evening Dickens unwound from the day by taking off his shoes as he read and smoked. With his socked foot he would stroke Mrs. Bouncer for an hour or so.

> He had a peculiar voice and way of speaking for her, which she knew perfectly well and would respond to at once. … To be stroked with a foot had great fascination for Mrs. Bouncer … ("Charles Dickens at Home," New York Times, 6 April 1884)

Dickens's bond with Mrs. Bouncer was very strong, dreaming of her when he was away from home. In a letter to his daughter, he says:

> "In my mind's eye I behold 'Mrs. Bouncer still with some traces of anxiety on her faithful countenance, balancing herself a little unequally on her forelegs, pricking up her ears with her head on one side, and slightly opening her intellectual nostrils. I send my loving and respectful duty to her."

To come full circle in understanding the importance of dogs in Dickens life, we can consider an actual physical landmark from his formative years.

> "My usual way home was over Blackfriars Bridge and down that turning in the Blackfriars Road which has Rowland Hill's chapel on one side, and the likeness of a golden dog licking a golden pot over a shop door on the other."

A twelve-year-old Charles Dickens passed by the Dog and Pot sign each day. At the time, his family was in a debtor's prison, and he felt painfully alone. Dickens' great-great-grandson Mark Dickens unveiled a replica of the sign in the Southward section of London on Dickens' 201st birthday. It may not be by an accident that the sign left an impression with young Dickens. The dog looks thin and is partaking of a meal from what Dickens describes as a golden pot. Did Dickens identify with the stray, his own Great Expectations in the work? Or was the dog an emblem of relief marking the end of the workday at a job he hated and carried with it a heavy emotional toll? In either case, the Dog and Pot sign may have laid the foundation for Dickens' fascination with dogs as an adult, a symbolic way to look back at those early years in a different, more manageable way.

Charles Dickens is remembered by many as a humanitarian presence within the context of the often-harsh 19th centuries' everyman's economic and cultural strains. But he was not a saint nor was he free from missteps in his many relations with people or pets. Instead, he was a very complex person. Claire Tomalin's biography of Dickens defines him with no less than 37 descriptors, among these were:

The child victim, the irrepressibly ambitious young man, the Reporter, the demonic worker, the tireless walker. The radical, the protector of orphans, helper of the needy, man of good works, the Republican. The giver of parties, the magician, the traveler. The satirist, the surrealist, the mesmerist. The angry son, the good friend, the bad husband, the quarreler, the sentimentalist, the secret lover, the despairing father. The player of games the lover of circuses, the country squire, the smoker, the drinker, the dancer of reels and hornpipes... Too mixed to be a gentleman- but wonderful.

Dickens was for sure a multifaceted person. Perhaps with all the complexity that made up who he was it was the elegant simplicity of the human-animal bond that appealed to Dickens. The type of least common denominator that our psyche craves.

For me, if Dickens was a character within one of his own novels, he might judge himself in part by how he sympathized with those who felt alone in the way he viscerally understood. That understanding is likely extended to animals as well. Perhaps in his best moments he would be portrayed as someone that encouraged the treatment of wayward beings, whether they are human or animal strays with understanding. He wanted us all to find a home.

Little Dog Boy

Sir Edwin Henry Landseer was the best known and the most beloved animal painter in the Victorian era. He grew up in a family of artists, his father John Landseer was a respected engraver. He was also Edwin's first teacher. John had a reputation for crankiness and foul moods, some of which may have been due to his deafness. He was known to gesture with his hearing horn, sometimes using it as a megaphone when wanting to emphasize a point to his sons. Painting class was held in the fields of Hampstead Heath. There Edwin and his two brothers would sketch the grazing animals.

The demanding tutelage of his father, combined with the hours spent observing animals, served young Edwin well as an artist. But his father's overbearing nature did not assist the person he was becoming. Edwin had his first work accepted to the Royal Academy at the age of eight. It was an engraved plate, the subject of course being animals - sheep and a boar. Henry Fuseli was Edwin's third teacher. He nicknamed him "little dog boy" for his knack of painting dogs.

Landseer is praised for the anatomical correctness of his animal subjects, but it was his ability to capture a dog's sentiment that would help change the way Victorian England regarded canine companions. The themes of a dog's steadfast loyalty and deep devotion even up to and beyond their master's death would be the theme of many of his most well-known paintings. The Poor Dog (or The Shepherd's Grave) in 1829 and The Old Shepherd's Chief Mourner in 1837 are among his most loved works. In these paintings Landseer sets the tone for dog lover's and the special attributes they see in their canine companions.

As an artist, Landseer grew to immense popularity. Queen Victoria owned no less than 39 of his paintings, many of whose subjects were her own dogs. Landseer even conducted sketching seminars for the Queen and Prince Albert. The middle class that could not afford an original Landseer had engravings of his work decorating their homes. Or as mentioned in the next chapter, even cheaper replicas could be obtained by the working class. But such success came with a high price. Landseer took on too many commissions which he had trouble completing. He sometimes went years before adding the finishing touches, that is, if they were completed at all. This created a situation where he dodged those asking for the completion dates of their works. The result was straining relations with society members, patrons and even the Queen. The tension was sometimes eased by Landseer's friends. He was known to be popular and charming with a good sense of humor.

One of his more well-known friends was the writer, Charles Dickens. While they met in the 1830's, Landseer had been a fan of Dickens' work for some time. In fact, Landseer read Oliver Twist to his colleagues at the Royal Academy. Doing this incurred the wrath of his cranky father who even used the hearing horn in megaphone fashion to inquire what Landseer was reading. Upon realizing the book in question was not about painting but instead "Dickens nonsense" his father instructed him to waste no further time on "such stuff."

Landseer and Dickens shared a keen interest in animals. Before Dickens' dog days, he kept a raven of which Landseer remarked he would not stop talking about. When Dickens needed to depart for a long trip to the Continent, Landseer volunteered to pet sit Dickens' second raven and eagle. Landseer even illustrated a dog for one of Dickens' works, A Cricket on the Hearth.

Another aspect that cemented the friendship was a shared sense of humor. Landseer was visiting Dickens who at the time was sitting for a portrait. Dickens was showing off his newly grown beard and mustache. Charles asked Landseer what he thought of his new appearance. Landseer replied, "A great improvement…it hides most of your face." Landseer and Dickens always remained friends but as they both grew older the pair began to drift apart. Each had their own worries to manage.

The artist suffered most of his life from anxiety that at times was debilitating. Not unrelated, was a growing dependency on alcohol and drugs to calm himself. He aged quickly, often seeming in a fragile state. Charles Dickens commented upon his rough state in these latter years, stating Landseer had aged quickly. At one point, the Landseer' family had Edwin committed to a psychiatric hospital in July 1872. After his release he found some relief by returning to his first love, nature. Spending the day observing animals in the field seemed to sooth him.
Sir Edwin Landseer died in 1873. But not before he was elected to full honors at the Royal Academy, and then later knighted in 1850. His passing was honored with the lowering of both flags to half-mast and having blinds drawn in windows. There was also hanging of wreaths around the bronze lions he designed in 1867 for legendary British Naval Admiral Horatio Nelson's monument in Trafalgar Square. This was a farewell befitting a man that brought a special sentiment to the 19th century dog lovers and beyond. A touching ending for a Little Dog Boy.

Fidelity

This entry is different from the rest found in the book in that it is a story within a story involving a painting with two separate lives. Each has a similar theme emphasizing the steadfast nature of a dog.

Briton Riviere was one of Victorian England's most popular 19th century painters often utilizing dogs as his subjects. As we will see in a later chapter, his work was also used by Charles Darwin to illustrate animal's emotional expressions. Riviere's 1869 painting, pictured above, interestingly has two titles. It was originally called "Prisoners" depicting a young poacher and his dog awaiting trial in a barren prison cell.

The painting was later acquired by William Hesketh Lever (also known later as Lord Leverhulme). Lever began manufacturing soap in England in 1884. He built Britain's largest company on the Lux brand, Latin for "sun." He referred to the brand as Sunlight Soap. Unlike the 19th-20th century Robber Barons of the United States, Lord Leverhulme prioritized his workers' welfare. He built a plant and community near Liverpool called Port Sunlight. In comparison to the overcrowded slums that were prevalent in the day, Lever's workers had homey cottages. These well-appointed homes had exposed timber ceilings, windows, running water, and indoor bathrooms. Schools were also built to educate the workers 500 children living in the community. In a time when women suffragettes marched for equal rights, Port Sunlight also offered special educational/ vocational classes for women and girls. By 1909, the community had a theatre, concert hall, a library, a gymnasium and a swimming pool. Lever was considered a friend of the working man.

Lever was also a pioneer in utilizing advertising to promote his brand. Lever started collecting art on behalf of Sunlight Soap. Lever went to art exhibitions in London and bought pictures which he thought would appeal to his customers. Each piece of art was woven into advertising campaigns for his product. The approach served dual purposes. First, it set the tone for his product. Secondly, the art in the ads became inexpensive ways to decorate working class homes. Soap wrappers contained vouchers that could be collected and exchanged for prints.

While Lever's interest in art seemed to have started for business reasons, later he developed his own taste much of which is housed today in the permanent collection located at Lady Lever Art Gallery, named in memory of his wife. It is also where one could find Briton Riviere's painting with two titles. In one of Lever's more successful ad campaigns each individually wrapped Sunlight Soap bars were accompanied by the catchphrase, "Lux Won't Shrink Woolens." Also, wrapped into the Sunlight Soap campaign, was the painting formerly known as "Prisoners" now reintroduced as "Fidelity." It capitalized upon the steadfastness of the dog for his master, a comparison that was not lost upon the public looking for a trustworthy brand of soap. The success of the campaign increased sales from 10,000 cases in 1915 to over 1 million cases in 1918.

My fellow sufferer

"Life is a wretched business. I've decided to spend my
life trying to understand it."
Arthur Schopenhauer

The German philosopher Arthur Schopenhauer (1788–1860) was a renowned curmudgeon. Growing up as the son of a merchant he was groomed to follow in his father's footsteps. However, with his father's death the younger Schopenhauer gained the financial security to pursue philosophy as a career goal. Schopenhauer was a complex man, and his formative years reflect how this came to be.

Arthur's father was severely depressed. Making matters worse, the senior Schopenhauer was married to a much younger woman. She had a very different, more lively temperament. When Schopenhauer's father eventually committed suicide, Arthur blamed his mother for not honoring his father's memory. The now seventeen year-old had become an angry young man. He quarreled bitterly with his mother. His mother in return had difficulty dealing with her moody and argumentative son as she states herself:

"It is necessary for my happiness to know that you are happy, but not to be a witness of it."

Schopenhauer seemed to transfer his ambivalent if not hostile feelings from his mother to other women. He never married and his love-life brought him little happiness. Arthur never knew the experience of reciprocated love by a woman.

Professionally, Schopenhauer was a clear insightful writer, but also unfortunately a self-destructive force that sabotaged his own cause. He once entered an essay contest sponsored by the Royal Danish Society of Scientific Studies. While his was the only entry, it was nonetheless rejected. It seems he went too far attacking his rival philosopher Georg Wilhelm Friedrich Hegel. Hegel offered in direct comparison to Schopenhauer an optimistic view of humanity. He also had quite a large following, especially at the university where both he and Schopenhauer lectured.

Schopenhauer purposefully set his lectures at the same time as Hegel's, only to be deeply disappointed by the few students in attendance. In some cases, he even lectured to an empty classroom. In keeping with his characteristic approach, Schopenhauer dealt with the Royal Danish Society essay contest and his rival in a similar way. He eventually self-published the essay submitted for the contest, promoting it as the one 'Not awarded a prize by the Royal Danish Society of Scientific Studies.' He also added a preface containing more abuse for Hegel. And not to be overlooked there were a few jabs for the Royal Danish Society as well. While work and love were two areas in which Schopenhauer struggled, his most satisfying relationships were with animals, especially dogs.

In 1851, Schopenhauer wrote his essay, 'On the Suffering of the World.' This piece discussed the inevitable difficulties we all face, but for some who read it they were surprised by how he also included not just the suffering of humans but also that of non-humans as well. The latter's misfortunes are illustrated by the image of a chained dog:

> "Never do I see such a dog without feelings of the deepest sympathy for him and of profound indignation against his master. I think with satisfaction of a case, reported some years ago in the Times, where a lord kept a large dog on a chain. One day as he was walking through the yard, he took it into his head to go and pat the dog, whereupon the animal tore his arm open from top to bottom, and quite right too! What he meant was this: 'You are not my master, but my devil, who makes a hell of my brief existence!' May this happen to all who chain up dogs."

Several Schopenhauer's contemporaries downplayed or even dismissed his concern for dogs.

They referred to the concern as Schopenhauer's "hobby horse" , a subject that someone speaks or complains about too often.

Schopenhauer was well-known for being an uber-cynic turning his back on humanity. In fact, he is characterized as the most prominent pessimist in the entire Western philosophical tradition, believing suffering and misfortune are the general rule in life. According to Schopenhauer the best one can hope for is to adjust expectations accordingly, that life should be viewed in terms of serving time in a penal colony. It may not seem too out of place then that Schopenhauer encourages us all to address one another not as "Sir" or "Mam" but instead as "my fellow sufferer." Ironically, he believes that there is a benefit to this view of life, encouraging us to develop tolerance and patience for our fellowman, recognizing everyone stands in need, struggling with similar misfortunes. Schopenhauer message of suffering is juxtaposed to that of the great comfort he found in the company of his dogs saying:

> "Whoever has never kept dogs does not know what it is to love and be loved."

He also owned a series of poodles naming them all "Atma." The name was inspired from the Hindu word for the universal soul from which all other souls arise. Quite a compliment to his canine companions. His favorite "Atma" came towards the end of his life. To this brown poodle, he bequeathed funds to ensure that the dog would be properly cared for the remainder of his life. During Schopenhauer's lifetime he was known to have portraits of his dogs rotated for viewing on the walls of his apartment.

What may ring true for many is Schopenhauer's view of the world being experienced in difficult terms. Yet the exception to the rule is the company we keep with animal companions. But you do not have to be a full-fledged curmudgeon, to know the power of the bond. Even those with satisfied lives know they have found something unique when spending time with an animal friend.

A Difference of Degree and Not Kind

"If we choose to let conjecture run wild, then animals, our fellow brethren in pain, diseases, death, suffering and famine – our slaves in the most laborious works, our companions in our amusements – they may partake our origin in one common ancestor – we may be all netted together." –
Charles Darwin: A passage from one of Darwin's journals as a young man

The naturalist Charles Darwin is best known for developing the theory of evolution. What is less recognized is that Darwin though an extremely productive writer and scientist, was also a recluse for nearly thirty years in his adult life. The reason being he suffered from almost constant illness. Symptoms included gastro-intestinal pains resulting in Darwin being flatulent, especially in the evening. There were also heart palpitations, hyperventilation, and fears he was going to die or go mad. Emotionally, he experienced periods of depressive feelings and uncontrollable weeping.

Some have argued that Darwin had an undiagnosed case of what is known today as Chagas's Disease involving cardiac and intestinal problems. Triatomine bugs also called the "kissing bugs" emerge from the walls of a dirt or adobe home for a nocturnal feeding. Unfortunately, the late-night snacks are often on people's faces as they sleep. Adding insult to injury the bugs bite and ingest the human's blood, only to then defecate on the person. The transmission of the disease occurs when the feces enter the body through mucous membranes or cuts in the skin. Darwin recorded in his journal that while in Argentina as a part of his five-year voyage on the HMS Beagle he was bitten by an insect that some have concluded was the kissing bug. But others have noted from the journals Darwin kept his symptoms were present long before the incident.

Instead of creepy-crawly reasons for symptoms, psychoanalyst John Bowlby suggested in a biography of Darwin more psychological causes. Bowlby meticulously reconstructs Darwin's life story including the exploration of his family and the previous generations' approach to dealing with the untimely deaths of children, spouses, and parents. Bowlby offers that Darwin's medical condition is a psychosomatic illness beginning with the death of Charles' mother when he was eight years old. While the Darwin family were certainly not alone in dealing with losses, there are certain conditions that make the surviving individuals susceptible to anxiety and depression. Bowlby suggests Darwin inherits a type of "vulnerable personality" derived from familial elements. Various relatives on both sides of Darwin's family tree suffered from gloomy and nervous symptoms. Then there was the family's stoic approach to loss that did not allow for grieving. In fact, young Charles was told by his sisters and father they should never speak of his mother again. His father who was a larger-than-life man literally and figuratively, making it abundantly clear that men did not give way to emotions.

One episode stands out on how the prescribed approach to loss impacts young Charles. He begins taking long solitary walks in the woods after this mother's passing. In one case he is so absorbed in his own thoughts he stumbles off the side of the road and falls eight feet. Much later in Darwin's autobiography he also shares that while he was eight years old at the time of his mother's death, he can remember almost nothing of her. The inability to access the tangible recollection of his mother is important in our understanding of Darwin.

Bowlby suggests it was unprocessed grief that would linger throughout Darwin's life. The metaphor he offers is a type of "secret cupboard" where Darwin tried to keep the pain of grief locked out of sight and out of mind. Adding this approach was Darwin's intense work ethic. Being a work alcoholic allows one to stay busy and offers a distraction from unwanted feelings. Additional support for Bowlby's psychosomatic thesis was Darwin's attacks reoccurred when members of his family died, or when he was trying to comfort friends dealing with loss. In these cases, the intensity of the symptoms left Darwin incapacitated. Bowlby suggests in these instances, Darwin's secret cupboard creaked open mixing current losses with very old ones. Charles became overwhelmed and his body expressed the emotional pain he felt.

While the secret cupboard keeps feelings of sadness and loss contained, so too where other emotions such as anger kept in check. Darwin preferred to do the writing and research while having others fight the more public battles for his theories. Leaving others to be his front men kept Darwin out of many heated clashes concerning evolution. What was not so tightly reined in were feelings of self-reproach. Darwin was highly sensitive to other's criticism seeming to take any wayward comment, especially from an authority figure as the truth. Darwin shares his method of dealing with the resulting self-incrimination. He repeats to himself one hundred times he did the best that he could, and no person could expect more.

While Darwin is celebrated for his famous text on evolution, "Origin of Species," published in 1859, we also want to consider themes that occurred in later books, "The Descent of Man" and "The Expression of the Emotions in Man and Animals." In these books, Darwin claimed human and non-human animals shared a common ancestor. While viewed as very controversial at the time, there were numerous implications from Darwin's work that impacts how many of us regard our animal companions today. Darwin suggested in "The Descent of Man" that man and higher order mammals differ by "degree and not kind." That is, while we may vary in terms of some aspects our experience in the world, we also share certain commonalities. An example of this type of universality is explored in "The Expression of the Emotions" emphasizing a common set of emotions and accompanying facial expressions. In his book, Darwin was among the first to use photographs in a scientific manuscript. In this case photos to illustrate the human varieties of emotional expressions. However, for the animals he depicted, Darwin turned to Victorian artists to capture their expressions. Among those that contributed to the book was Briton Riviere (Fidelity). The illustration above is one found in Darwin's book illustrating a dog expressing fear. The image was modeled after Darwin's favorite dog Polly.

In many people's thinking, Darwin may be more strongly associated with monkeys than dogs, but he had a special connection with canines all his life. His father once commented in a sharp way (which Darwin never forgot) that young Charles was not much of a go-getter and seemed to be mostly concerned with dogs and hunting. As an adult, Darwin found ways to incorporate what he learned from canine companionship into his scientific work. He even begins the argument for evolution in "The Descent of Man" by discussing the greyhound as an example of an adaptive species that has straddled the two worlds of the domestic and wild. Domestication is what helped the dog adapt and survive through a strong bond with humankind. The notion would later influence ethnologists and psychologists believing mankind's bond with animals, especially dogs, also played a key role in human being's own survival of the species. One of the reasons being mankind and dog have a long-shared history seemingly hardwired for each other's company.

While dogs played a role professionally, they also touched Darwin's life personally. It was a terrier named Polly that would capture Darwin's heart in the last decade of his life. Polly sat in her basket beside Darwin as he wrote at his desk. His wife Emma shed some light on how this bond began, that in the aftermath of Polly losing a litter of puppies, she became completely devoted to Dr. Darwin. Emma continues that Polly seems to believe Darwin to be "a very big puppy," licking his hands, and becoming distressed when made to be apart.

One of Darwin's closest colleagues English biologist Thomas Henry Huxley poked fun at Polly's elevated status calling her the "Ur-hund" or idealized type of dog. To drive home his point, Huxley also drew Polly's imagined evolutionary tree, including an equal measure of pigs and cats. In her defense, Darwin's daughter Henrietta exclaimed that Polly was remarkable for her beauty of character not so much for that of her appearance.

Interesting enough, the last ten years of Darwin's life took a turn for the better. His symptoms that had been so prevalent for thirty years, went into a type of remission. This occurrence leaves Charles freer that seemingly ever before. There is no doubt several factors aided Darwin's improvement. As Bowlby notes in his biography, Darwin's controversial theory of evolution finally won him a long list of accolades, ones he longed for but at the same time was too painfully modest to pursue. The praise may have also diminished the feared criticism of his work, reducing Darwin's own anxiety. It is also curious that work associated with writing the book, "The Expression of the Emotions in Man and Animals" occurred during this period. It would seem to be just the right anecdote for a person who needed an intellectual way of approaching and understanding feelings. Perhaps as he wrote the presence of his dog Polly also provided for him an experience Darwin had needed since the formative years. While Emma Darwin points out Polly saw Darwin as her big pup, it may be a stretch to claim this was akin to the maternal presence Charles was cheated out of as a child. But if we think it terms of a 'difference of degree and not kind' applied to having emotional needs met, perhaps an animal companion can even help with unmet needs in a significant way. It makes one wonder if the long hours spent writing in his study were attempts to not only work on his theories but also work through some of the emotional residual of losses accrued over his life. In this case, part of what possibly occurred was an unlocking of his secret cupboard aided by the caring and attentive presence of Polly. Darwin's belief in the kinship of humans and non-human animals lead to new insights. He wrote, 'is as plain and almost as pathetic as in the case of our children'. Man himself could not express love and humility 'so plainly as does a dog, when with drooping ears…wagging tail, he meets his beloved master'.

Darwin knew firsthand of the experience of which he wrote. Polly was a devoted companion to the end, outliving her master by only a few days. She was buried under an apple tree near the Darwin's home.

A New Book
BY RUDYARD KIPLING

THE JUNGLE BOOK

Published by THE CENTURY Co.

For Sale Here ··· Price $1.50

The First Friend

Nobel Prize winning author Rudyard Kipling was born in India in 1865. He later came to England as a young child. He is perhaps best remembered for his children's books like, "The Jungle Book." Animals have a strong presence in many of his works. He was also known as an avid and unapologetic dog lover. Beneath his well-known prickly persona Kipling felt deeply for dogs. Kipling especially liked the Aberdeen terrier breed. One such dog occasionally made a camo appearance as a character or narrator in his stories. "Thy Servant a Dog" published in 1930 contains three tales told from the perspective of Boots, son of Kildonan Brogue, champion reserve.

One may explain Kipling fascination with animals in part through his creative mind that was evident at a young age. Some of the other forces that would also shape his formative years made a bond with animals an indispensable whether they were in real or in imagined form.

In Kipling's autobiography he details the difficulties he experienced as a child. When "Ruddy" was five and his sister Trix was three, their parents brought them by ship from India to England. In the first chapter of his autobiography, "A Very Young Person" Kipling discusses his experience being placed in the care of the Sea Captain and Mrs. Holloway, who ran a boarding house for the children of British parents residing in India. Kipling described these years as the unhappiest of his life. He made up stories to alleviate the anxiety he felt when Mrs. Holloway's perfectionism and overzealous religious attitudes overwhelmed him. Of those six years spent with the couple, Kipling wondered if the mixture of cruelty and neglect might have formed the foundation of his literary writing skills:

> "If you cross-examine a child of seven or eight on his day's doings (specially when he wants to go to sleep) he will contradict himself very satisfactorily. If each contradiction be set down as a lie and retailed at breakfast, life is not easy. I have known a certain amount of bullying, but this was calculated torture—religious as well as scientific. Yet it made me give attention to the lies I soon found it necessary to tell: and this, I presume, is the foundation of literary effort."

There is also another aspect to mention regarding Kipling's background and that involved his only son John. For many, Kipling became synonymous as the voice for Great Britain in its heyday of an imperial power where the sun never set on its borders. He burst with pride when John wanted to serve in World War I. However, he was disqualified from service in the navy due to poor eyesight. Kipling pulled strings and helped John receive a commission in the infantry. Shortly after John's

18th birthday his regiment was sent to what is now known as the Battle of Loos. It was there that under heavy German machine gun fire it is believed John lost his life. However, his body was not recovered. Kipling attempted for four years to ascertain his son's whereabouts. Kipling interviewed men from John's battalion and wrote to senior military officials. He even contacted the Red Cross and neutral ambassadors in Sweden hoping they could make inquiries of German officials, asking if John's body had been found. In 1919 Kipling exhausting his lines of inquiry wrote a letter to the army accepting his son was dead.

After John's death Kipling was a changed man. He publicly grew bitter about the World War and privately wrote about grief. Jan Montefiore, professor of 20th Century English Literature at University of Kent suggests that Kipling contributed hugely to the "literature of mourning." Some of his works are directly connected to soldier's deaths such as the poem "My Boy Jack" about a16-year-old sailor Jack Cornwell that lost his life in the war. Other works combine elements of loss in a soldier's life with the presence of a beloved dog. Some efforts are directly about dog's place in our life and the pain that is felt when they are lost.

There are many of Kipling stories from which to choose that illustrates not only his love of dogs but their special place in our lives. I have selected just three. It is interesting to note that later in Kipling's life after his daughter married and it was just, he and his wife Carrie, a line of Aberdeen terriers kept him company as he wrote. In 1930, he published "Thy Servant the Dog." The book takes the unusual approach of having a canine narrator for the first three tales. Boots, a black Aberdeen terrier has a simple command of language but a limited understanding of all the events occurring. The literary technique provides a playful way for readers to engage but the approach was panned by some critics - 'Few major writers have written so bad a book: almost none in their maturity.' Such criticism did not seem to impact the public's view. Thy Servant the Dog went on to record sales.

Even in other stories in Thy Servant the Dog when a dog is not the narrator, the focus is clearly on the power of dogs in our lives. In one such story, "Garm – a Hostage," the human narrator finds his friend Private Stanley Ortheris off the military base acting in a drunk and disorderly fashion, on the verge of being arrested. The narrator takes Stanley home, and devises an excuse to get him safely back on base the next morning. As an act of supreme gratitude, Stanley gifts his dog Garm to his friend. Garm is bullterrier, pure white, with a fawn-coloring. Garm proves to be an exceptional dog, highly intelligent and brave, saving the narrator's dog from a pack of ferocious strays. While the narrator nicknames Garm the 'Bloody Breast,' he then glimpses the more tender side of why Private Stanley Ortheris values him so much. And unbeknown to the narrator, Stanley secretly comes to visit Garm several times a week. Both Ortheris and Guam becomes sadder and weaker the longer they are apart. The solder's condition worsens, and he is sent off to convalesce in the hills. Garm is also afflicted by intense grief for his former master. From a consultation with a doctor the narrator is told, "He's (Garm) dying of a broken heart." The narrator realizing there is only one way to mend the situation. He tracks Stanley down with dog in tow. The private agrees to take Garm back, and they are happily reunited. It is Kipling's unique and evocative writing style that best captures that moment when loss gives way to reunion.

He flew through the air bodily, and I heard the whack of him as he flung himself at Stanley, knocking the little man clean over. They rolled on the ground together, shouting, and yelping, and hugging. I could not see which was dog and which was man, till Stanley got up and whimpered.

There is also the well-known Kipling's poem, "The Power of the Dog." This verse speaks to the deep feelings many have regarding the loss of their animal companion.

There is sorrow enough in the natural way

From men and women to fill our day;

And when we are certain of sorrow in store,

Why do we always arrange for more?

Brothers and sisters, I bid you beware

Of giving your heart to a dog to tear.

Of Kipling's works that include a dog, my favorite is taken from, "The cat that walked by himself." The story is an Adam and Eve-type origin tale occurring "when the tame animals were wild." The first man and woman send out invitations to all the animals in the "wild wet woods" to come and join the newly formed domesticated family consisting of man and wife. The stubborn cat refuses the invitation unlike other animals from the "wild woods." The cat's point of view is this pact with mankind is the ultimate submission. But the dog sees things in a different way. The dog will be the first friend.

When the Man waked up he said, 'What is Wild Dog doing here?' And the Woman said, 'His name is not Wild Dog any more, but the First Friend, because he will be our friend for always and always and always.

Kipling's animal stories have an arguable archetypal quality and still speak to many readers today. One might contend that he hits upon both an element of pure love and grief. This tandem of emotions is among the most powerful of feelings because they lack ambivalent emotions. All that is retained is a pureness of connection whether it involve the first hello or saying goodbye to a steadfast friend. These are sentiments unencumbered by mixed feelings that dominate so many of our other relationships, even the good ones.

For me, Kipling will be the one that introduced the notion that an animal from wild woods will be forever linked with mankind as the first friend. It is a bond we have shared for more than 10,000 years - a successful long-term relationship by any standard.

Section II: Underdogs

The word "underdog" has several potential linguistic origins. One comes from the old maritime work of shipbuilding. Ship's floors were hand sawn from logs. The logs were placed on planks of wood that were called "dogs". The senior sawsman stood on top of the plank and he was the overdog. The junior had to go into the pit where he got covered in sawdust. He was the "underdog". The word underdog can also be traced to the 19th century's unsavoury occurrence of dogfighting, denoting which canine was likely to be beaten.

Nowadays the term underdog refers to people in various arenas of endeavour - sports, politics, and those that come from humble origins. Not all these folks were born in a log cabin or some modern-day equivalent, but it is perceived that fortune has not been kind for the underdog in question. In terms of the odds for success, fate is stacked against them and are not likely to prevail. Yet, giving someone the underdog designation can embolden one with a can-do spirit. A hope that someone can and will beat the odds through their own dogged

69

determination. Examples of such underdogs are numerous ranging from the little train that could, to a come from nothing everyman, to those that on one level have familial resources but lack parental love. In each of these cases, we do not expect the underdog to succeed, nor do we hold it against them if they do not. In fact, they seem the most human of characters for giving it a shot, when most everyone already knew the eventual outcome.

A recent series of studies concerning underdogs in political, and sports scenarios found participants in the study consistently rooted for and often favored the underdog to win. The researchers suggested that those who are viewed as disadvantaged pull for people's sense of fairness and justice. Another explanation for why people like underdogs more is because they work harder to overcome the odds. It has been suggested a key element of who the public regards as heroic are directly tied to being an underdog.

Some fortunate underdogs are also paired with canine companions. In some cases, this involves at-risk youth working with rescue dogs. The youth help the dogs become more adoptable through training, but the kids benefit as well. Recent studies have found that boys in these types of programs increase their emotional intelligence, and decrease the problem behaviors leading them to be in trouble.

The combination of one type of underdog helping another is hard to beat. It potentially speaks to a more universal quality of knowing what it means to feel vulnerable and seeing in the underdog duo the chance to vicariously experience overcoming the odds. In this section of the book, we see examples of how dogs make a difference even when no one thought it possible; perhaps not even the underdogs themselves.

The one absolutely unselfish friend

George Graham Vest (1830-1904) served as U.S. Senator from Missouri between the years of 1879 to 1903. He was one of the leading orators of his day. Vest is also responsible for one of our most beloved sayings taken from his closing arguments in a court hearing over the wrongful shooting of a dog. The speech has become known as a 'Tribute to the Dog." The phrase in question is – 'man's best friend.' Vest was someone that had a flair for the dramatic in his oratory style and found himself the underdog in more than one court or political showdown.

Before his days in the US Senate, Vest attended law school in Kentucky. Upon completion his plan was to head west to California with his family. However, he made a stopover in Missouri to successfully defend a slave accused of murder. After the acquittal, Vest was warned to leave the territory. But in keeping with his style, he decided instead to stay, setting up his legal practice. Personally, Vest was a man of slight build standing 5'6 and weighing in at mere 110 pounds. Vest's nickname was the "Little giant," a term given to him by loving friends who admired his personal prowess and a spirit much bigger than his physical size.

In the now famous Old Drum trail, Vest sought damages on behalf of his client Charles Burden whose dog, Old Drum, was shot by a neighbor. Old Drum was well-known in the local area. He was an excellent tracker and remembered as a strong and fearless presence. But it should be known that he was given his name based on the unique quality of his voice. The dog had a deep sound, like that made when striking a drum. The accused in the trial of Old Drum was not only Burden's neighbor but also his brother-in-law, Leonidas Hornsby. Hornsby believed that wandering dogs had been killing his sheep. He made threats to shoot any dog that stepped on his property. Although Hornsby had hunted with Old Drum, and acknowledged him to be an excellent dog, he also suspected the dog was one of the sheep poachers. Hornsby carried out his threat one night as he found Old Drum prowling in his yard. Hornsby ordered one of his hired hands to shoot him.

Burden sued Hornsby for damages. The trial quickly became the talk of the county if not the state. Each man was determined to win the case and hired the best attorneys available. Technically the case was docketed as Burden vs. Hornsby, but was known as "The Drum Case." After several trials in lower courts followed by appeals from the loser, the case finally reached the Supreme Court of Missouri in Johnson City. Rather than discussing the details of the case, Vest eloquently praised the loyal nature of a dog that brought tears to the eyes of the jury. The senior partner of the law firm for the defendant was Thomas T. Crittenden, later the Governor of Missouri. In an interview shortly after Senator Vest's death, Crittenden gave his recollections of the case.

"I have often heard him but never have I heard from his lips, nor from those of any other man, so graceful, so impetus and so eloquent a speech as Vest's before the jury in that dog case. He seemed to recall from history all the instances where dogs had displayed intelligence and fidelity to man. He quoted more lines of history and poetry about them than I had supposed had been written, capping the monument he had erected by quotations from the Bible of dogs soothing the sores of Lazarus, from Byron's "Tis sweet to hear the honest watchdog's bark,' from Scott's…It was as perfect a piece of oratory as ever was heard from pulpit or bar. Court, jury, lawyers and audience were entranced. I looked at the jury and saw all were in tears, especially the foreman, who wept copiously as one who has lost his best friend…Drum has been canonized by that speech in that part of Missouri. When Vest left the court house, even the dogs of the village seemed to gather around him in their love and followed him as their friend to his hotel."

While no record was kept of the last half of Vest's tribute to a dog, the first portion fortunately was preserved. It was this speech that originated the saying, "A man's best friend is his dog." The following is an excerpt from the speech given on October 18, 1869 at the trial:

Gentlemen of the jury:… The one absolutely unselfish friend that a man can have in this selfish world, the one that never deserts him and the one that never proves ungrateful or treacherous is his dog….A man's dog stands by him in prosperity and in poverty, in health and in sickness….If fortune drives the master forth an outcast in the world, friendless and homeless, the faithful dog asks no higher privilege than that of accompanying him to guard against danger, to fight against his enemies, and when the last scene of all comes, and death takes the master in its embrace and his body is laid away in the cold ground, no matter if all other friends pursue their way, there by his graveside will the noble dog be found, his head between his paws, his eyes sad but open in alert watchfulness, faithful and true even to death (Morrow 2012, p. 290).

The award of $50 in damages (the maximum allowed by law) was given to Burden for the loss of Old Drum. During the trial, Vest stated that he would "win the case or apologize to every dog in Missouri." No apologies needed Senator…

The Runt

Thomas Sayers was an English 19th century bare-knuckles prize fighter. In 1860, he was considered the British champion. By some estimates, also the first World Boxing Champion, or at least he fought to a draw with the then American champion, John Camel Heenan. That was quite a feat for this underdog. The David versus Goliath championship event caused quite a stir on both sides of the Atlantic.

In his championship fight with Heenan, Tom gave away forty pounds and five inches in height to a much larger and younger rival. Sayers weighed in at a meager 150 pounds. Tom was accustomed to being out matched physically, but in previous fights he defeated much larger opponents. This was a time in boxing history before weight classes. So, mismatched opponents could square off bare knuckled against each other.

In a time when fights could go on for hours and include seconds to back up each fighter, Tom lost the toss regarding which side of the makeshift ring he called home base. Boxing rings usually consisted of a circle of onlookers, not a physical structure seen in modern boxing. With the sun in his face, the melee went on for 37 rounds of bare-knuckle brawling. Tom was knocked down several times, and injured his arm, leaving him to box at one point single handed.

Tensions were very high for supporters of both boxers. That was not entirely out of love and admiration for one's champion. Large sums of money could be won, and sometimes violent brawls ensued after the matches between rival wagers. As Tom battled on, finally, the crowd erupted and stormed the ring. The referee tried to end the contest, but the ring was reformed, and the boxers went on for another 4 or 5 more rounds of very shaky fisticuffs before it was stopped. Given boxing was illegal at the time, though still covered by the newspapers, the riot act kept the whereabouts of matches secret. In this case, the contest was only concluded when police got wind of the bout and onlookers scattered. The battle royale was declared a drawl.

After the Heenan fight of 1860, Tom Sayers never fought again. Funds were raised for him to support his retirement from boxing. In his post-boxing years, Tom briefly worked for, and eventually bought a circus. Unfortunately, "Tom Sayers' Champion Circus" was about as worn thin as Tom himself. Within two years it was auctioned off.

After retirement Sawyer fell on further hard times, it is said that as his health began to fade so did his good-natured temperament. What tuberculosis and diabetes did not claim, alcoholism absorbed the rest. There were also tensions with his estranged wife regarding the rightful father of their three children, and who was eligible to inherit his estate. Sayers died at the age of 39. However, the difficult end of life circumstances did not dampen the celebration of his accomplishments. It has been estimated that over 100,000 people attended his funeral. Spectator magazine stated that the crowd accompanying Tom's remains stretched for more than two miles. Four ponies pulled his coffin. Sitting alone in the pony cart was Tom's chief mourner - his Mastiff dog named Lion. Many of his friends remembered vividly Sayers driving his horse drawn carriage up and down the streets with his Bull Mastiff at his side. Tom Sayers is buried in Highgate Cemetery where his marble tomb is guarded by the stone image of Lion, his beloved dog that now rests forever beside his master.

There is a special connection between dogs and human underdogs. Perhaps it is based upon the grounding experience of having someone squarely in your corner.

His Master's Voice

Nipper the dog achieved the status of a cultural icon. The small but feisty Jack Russell has for more than 100 years been the mascot for a record label, a company going through various iterations and known today as RCA Records.

Nipper received his name due to his tendency to nip the backs of guests' legs. When his first master Mark Barraud died in 1887, his brother Francis adopted Nipper taking him to his Liverpool, England home. Like his brother, Francis was also an artist, but he especially liked creating animal paintings.

Francis discovered that Nipper had a fascination with his phonograph, the early cylinder recording and playing machine. Francis "often noticed how puzzled he (Nipper) was to make out where the voice came from." While there are various versions of the story, it was the recordings of his former master Mark's voice that especially got Nipper's attention. He seemed to be looking for Mark in the horn of the Phonograph. Nipper, having heard Mark's voice, half-cocked his ears, with his face turned down attempting to smell his way to his lost friend. That image of Nipper stayed with Francis. After Nipper died in 1895, Francis tenderly recollected Nipper's endearing habit with the phonograph. It even became the inspiration for his now famous painting. Francis would later say about the recollection, "It certainly was the happiest thought I ever had." While the painting was originally titled "His Master's Voice," Francis copyrighted it for commercial reasons as: "Dog looking at and listening to a Phonograph."

After a failed attempt to have his painting exhibited at The National Gallery, Francis tried to sell it to any phonograph or gramophone company that showed an interest. His potential clients included Thomas Edison, who upon seeing the painting flatly refused. He stated dogs did not listen to phonographs.

There was an eventual buyer but even that took some doing. William Barry Owen, the manager of Gramophone Company seemed to have mixed feelings about the painting. Complicating things was he liked the company's current logo: an angel etching. Despite all this, Owen decided to offer Barraud a business proposal. If he was willing to edit the painting to include one of their gramophone machines, the company would agree to buy the painting. After some tedious months of negotiation, a deal was struck. If one looked closely the original work still bore the remnants of its previous incarnation, the black phonograph horn being replaced with a golden one. The painting was sold for the sum of 50 pounds.

Then a stroke of luck occurred. In May of 1899, Emile Berliner, the inventor of the gramophone and founder of the Gramophone Company visited the company's London office. He took notice of the painting hanging in Owen's office. Berliner contacted Barraud and requested a copy. Berliner then brought it to America, and with the help of his partner Eldridge Johnson, made Nipper the official trademark for the Victor Talking Machine Company.

Traveling around the world globe, Nipper's place was fixed among cultural icons, becoming the company official mascot for Victor Company in America, and HMV (short for "His Master's Voice") in Great Britain and JVC (Victor Company of Japan). Curiously, British Gramophone, the company that had first purchased the rights to the painting, would wait ten years before finally replacing their angel with Nipper as their primary trademark.

It is interesting to note that some considered Barraud's work ethic questionable. His nickname was Bumblebee, "because he was a chronic bumbler in everything he did." Even with that said, Barraud was commissioned to make additional copies and iterations of "His Master's Voice" over the years.

As for Nipper, what is known of him included a weakness for chasing rats, which cost him an eye as he ran into a thorn bush during an unsuccessful hunting episode. The original painting may have evoked a different sentiment if it included Nipper wearing a pirate's eye patch. In either case, "His Master's Voice" hangs in the offices of EMI, the successor of the Gramophone Company. It is one of the most widely recognized and valuable commercial trademarks. "His Master's Voice" also draws from a resounding Victorian theme of unending faithfulness amid grief. The idea had been personified by various animal painters of the era, especially for 19th century artists that utilized the dog.

Prince Hal

George Augustus Frederick, who would later be crowned George IV in 1820, remarked that being the heir apparent to the throne of England is not a position, but a predicament. The job duties include waiting for time to pass until eventually one ascends the throne. However, it is often the case that one makes the transition at an age when doing so is no longer desired. This includes the weighty responsibilities of the position becoming overwhelming even to a much younger man. George waited to be king until he was 58 years-old.

Another man that also knew something about the predicament of being the heir apparent was Albert Edward (November 9th 1841 – May 6th 1910). The man who was known affectionately as 'Bertie' would later be crowned King Edward VII in 1901. He was sixty years old before sitting upon the throne. That gave Bertie a good bit of time to kill, which he did in a grand and often decadent fashion. He was a dapper dresser, affable, and fond of many activities which his mother the queen did not approve of. The list was long and included: gambling, horse racing, affairs with beautiful married women, and overindulgence of food and drink.

At first glance it may seem unusual to place a royal in the underdog category. While diminutive physical stature or humble beginnings are the typical markers for underdogs, there is also another type that transcends one's physical appearance or social station in life. This type of underdog carries the moniker of being unlikely to succeed for different reasons. In this case it has to do with missing out on some of the essential emotional sustenance that is universally needed by all children – having a parent notice and believe in you. While this type of occurrence can appear in many scenarios, having a preoccupied and then grieving parent is among the most difficult for a child to deal with.

As an adult, King Edward VII ruled only nine years, but it has been argued that he was the most popular king of England since the early 1660s. He was also one of the last monarchs to have an impact on the grander scale of world affairs. However, his climb to mastering politics and diplomacy was not an easy one. In fact, some have compared Bertie to Shakespeare's Prince Hal from Henry the IV, the fun-loving boy prince that is not prepared to be the heir apparent, much less king. It is only when circumstances shift marked by death or tragedy does the boy begin his transition to becoming a man.

Bertie was a distracted boy that failed to capture the approval of either parent, something he badly desired. His response was one that many take – they rebel and become naughty children as a way of soliciting attention. When more pressure is applied as was the case with Bertie who was forced to study his lessons in isolation six days a week and up to ten hours a day, Bertie's behavior only worsened. For a brief time Bertie had a tutor that finally understood that he needed attention first and the rest would follow. But other advisors to his father Prince Albert suggested the pairing was too indulgent so Bertie even lost that connection.

Bertie was the son of Queen Victoria and her royal consort Albert. Albert was Victoria's love of her life, literally. Her children were a distant emotional second to that of her husband. Making matters worse for Bertie was his father Albert died prematurely at the young age of 42. Victoria spent the rest of her life in mourning. She wore black for the remainder of her life and avoided public appearances for many years. Her longing to bring Albert back showed itself in commissioned art and portraits of her husband. It also involved daily rituals that included having his clothing laid each morning, as if he still stood ready to dress. Or having a plate set for him at meals as though he was still there prepared to dine with The Queen. This type of preoccupied grieving does not favor the development of children and young adults who still need some form of parental support. It was likely the grief-stricken queen may have added to her inability to focus upon her son. There was also some inclination that Victoria emotionally blamed Bertie for her husband's death that it was brought on by worry over the Prince of Wales's philandering. He had been "killed by that dreadful business." She carried the opinion which was seconded by Albert when he was still alive, that Bertie would have difficulty amounting to much: "The poor country with such a terribly unfit, totally unreflecting successor!" The fun loving albeit somewhat emotionally wounded boy known as Bertie would one day as a man become king. I think it was fortunate that King Edward VII also was a dog lover.

Caesar (1898–1914) was a Wire Fox Terrier owned by King Edward VII. He was the King's constant companion. In case someone forgot or was unaware of this close arrangement, the dog wore a collar that read, "I am Caesar. I belong to the King." During his life Caesar had a personal footman assigned to him making sure he was neat and tidy. He was also allowed to sleep on a chair next to the King's bed. Caesar has been the subject of paintings, as well as the inspiration for children's stuffed animals and books. He even had a handcrafted hardstone model created in his likeness by the House of Fabergé.

Edward's last year's as king saw Great Britain mired in various cultural changes including social class conflict. There were mounting tensions for political and social reform. Perhaps out of habit or a way to relieve stress, Edward was a heavy smoker of cigarettes and twelve cigars a day. He also did not curb the collection of other voracious appetites. He was known to eat a full meal then bring a whole chicken to bed. Most mornings the chicken had been devoured. Towards the end of his life, Bertie increasingly suffered from bronchitis and on April 28, 1910, the king suffered several heart attacks. However, it is said, he refused to rest, saying, "No, I shall not give in; I shall go on; I shall work to the end." On May 6th, 1910, he passed away.

After The King's death, Caesar was accompanied by a highlander dressed in a kilt, walking behind the funeral carriage carrying The King's coffin. The dog walked in the procession in prominence ahead of dignitaries and heads of state that included nine kings.

The only one that voiced a complaint was Kaiser Wilhelm II of the German Empire.

Shortly after The King's death, a photograph taken by Thomas Heinrich Voigt of the elderly Edward VII sitting beside Caesar sold 100, 000 copies as postcards. Also, an unofficial book titled "Where's Master?" detailing Caesar's fictitious first-person account of the king's death up to the funeral. Apparently, the book did not sit well with the queen but was very popular with the public going through nine reprints the first year. After The King's death, a portrait of the Caesar entitled "Silent Sorrow" was painted by Maud Earl. In this work, Caesar is seen resting his head on The King's favorite chair.

Life after Bertie was initially challenging for Caesar. He sank into what appeared to dark period of mourning refusing to eat. He would spend time whining outside The King's bedroom until he managed one day to sneak in. He was later found by the queen hiding under The king's bed. The queen encouraged Caesar and eventually helped restore him to better health. Despite her previous dislike of the dog, the queen took interest in Caesar spoiling him with treats, confessing to a friend that she was making up for The King being so strict with him.

Caesar died following an operation in April 1914. The Fabergé figurine bearing his likeness is part of the permanent Royal Collection. Perhaps the most touching tribute to Caesar is that his likeness was sculpted with that of the king and queen atop their tomb in St George's Chapel, Windsor Castle. In the carving, Caesar lies at the feet of the king.

The little corporal & The grief of one dog

"To his dog, every man is Napoleon; hence the constant popularity of dogs".
–Aldous Huxley, 1894, English Novelist

Nineteen years after his death, Napoleon Bonaparte's remains are moved from the Island of Helena. The place of exile where he spent the last 6 years of his life in a rat infected, drafty house. He suffered from what is believed to be stomach cancer, enduring a long and painful death. But in death, his casket is brought through the city of Paris. Some believe it is finally safe to bring him home. A testament that nearly two decades after death, his memory still stirs excitement as well as fear. Loyalists and curious onlookers watch as he is entombed in a crypt under the church dome at Les Invalides in Paris. The chapel was originally part of a series of buildings serving old and unwell soldiers. Now a place of monuments housing the glorious dead. An earned place of rest after years of service. Napoleon's epitaph references the large dome atop of the church as a helmet befitting the giant nature of the one buried underneath it. This is quite a compliment for one who started life not as an aristocratic noble, nor an actual native son of France.

Napoleon was born instead on the island of Corsica shortly after France annexed the territory. Historians note that when Napoleon reached the mainland of France for the first time at age nine, he barely spoke any French. He also held in contempt those from privileged backgrounds that he encountered at the military school where he was enrolled as a scholarship student. These would be part of a series of events that would be pivotal in terms of shaping his future. One of his teachers noted that Napoleon was a loner and in some ways an outcast from the rest of the boys. Likely due to being from a different social class and language barriers. It also had something to do from the instructor's perspective that the young Napoleon, though certainly talented, was also egocentric, seemingly overestimating his own potential and importance.

Other roots of Napoleon's complex personality are multifaceted. Sigmund Freud traced his aggressive drive for ambition to his formative years. Napoleon saw his older brother Joseph as a rival for the position of the most favored son within the family. Given Freud was also the first son of his family, who also craved his parent's attention, his interpretation may be subject to some bias. In either case, simple generalizations would not be accurate or do justice in explaining his disposition.

Historians suggest he was mercurial and complex if not contradictory in nature. General Bonaparte could be inspiring and gentle with his soldiers, as well as, vindictive and callous with human life. As a young officer his troops nicknamed him "the little corporal" for his willingness to undertake dangerous acts of courage in battle more in keeping with a corporeal rather than the commanding general. The 'little' is not a reference to his size but rather an affectionate term showing he was loved by his troops.

And then how to categorize Napoleon's achievements? Was he a liberator, hero, or tyrant? Or perhaps a mix of all three. Confusing matters further was Bonaparte knew the art of impression management. Paintings were made to showcase his prowess some believing to hide a diminutive stature, or perhaps as a part of a positive spin campaign. He was known to falsify military documents to make himself look more heroic. Military campaigns that were disastrous were retold as victories. His image was purposefully adorned in mythological ways on gifts. They were sent to court favour of those he wished to impress. In other circumstances the same presents were sent to counter opposition, a type of imitation. Geoffrey Ellis concludes Napoleon has a unique ability to exploit situations to his advantage, reversing his course on the spot in an adaptive way.

A chameleon like nature served Napoleon well in politics but on a personal level. He often was restless, feeling alone most of his life. Napoleon obtained the recognition and power he so much desired, but he also met disappointment in those around him including his first marriage to Josephine. It was said he was crushed when finding she had been notoriously unfaithful. Some suggest his second marriage and aging, not to mention two involuntary exiles, either mellowed his nature or made him more forlorn, or perhaps both.

When Napoleon encountered setbacks, he seemed to find a resilient attitude upon many occasions. But throughout his adult life the disappointments of career and relationships sometimes left him despondent. He wrote to his brother a few times of stepping in front of a moving carriage if things did not improve. In his later years he withdrew further into himself.

Perhaps Napoleon is best understood in terms of a man who changed in some way over time as many of us do. Though more central elements like striving for achievement continued throughout his life. Even in exile he saw himself as ruler of the island implementing improvements in public works. He required those around him to formally dress for dinner as though exiles' reach was limited, only partially tarnishing former glory. Amid all this, there were occasions when an animal companion eased his pain or even inspired him.

An unnamed Newfoundland dog is credited for saving a drowning Napoleon Bonaparte in 1815. During his escape from exile on the island of Elba, rough seas knocked Napoleon overboard. Making matters worse, Napoleon did not know how to swim. Luckily for him a fisherman's dog jumped into the sea. The Newfoundland breed is especially known for their search and rescue ability. He kept the little corporal afloat until reaching safety. Of the experience Napoleon said: "Here, Gentlemen, a dog teaches us a lesson in humanity." This was not the only lesson he learned from a canine.

Very much in keeping with the theme of this book, while Napoleon had many interpersonal edges sometimes pushing others away (including creating a cult of personality and once commented that power was his mistress with ambitions to conquer the world), he also had a soft spot for dogs. Napoleon is known to have had at least two dogs, both were needed to weather the painful exile from the heyday of his career. While on Elba there was a dog called Lauro. Napoleon's dog on St Helena was called Sambo. Sambo whose ears were cut off in keeping with the fashion of the day, that left the dog resembling a seal. With that said, Napoleon was in possession of Sambo's ears until his death. After Napoleon's death in May 1821 the dog was taken back to Europe by Countess Bertrand and her children. Sambo is now a resident in the Musée de l'Armée in Paris, with his ears still missing.

Perhaps the most striking account of a dog offering a deep insight into who the man Napoleon was can be found as he slowly began his rise to power. In his journal, Napoleon Bonaparte also comments about the aftermath of a battle in 1796 where he encounters a dead soldier accompanied by his dog. The dog jumped from beneath the soldier's body, alternatively licking his face and howling.

> It was a beautiful, calm, moonlight night. Suddenly a dog, which had been hiding under the clothes of a dead man, came up to us with a mournful howl, and then disappeared again immediately into his hiding place. He would lick his master's face, then run up to us again, only to return once more to his master. Whether it was the mood of the moment, whether it was the place, the time, the weather, or the action itself, or whatever it was, it is certainly true that nothing on any battlefield ever made such an impression

on me. I involuntarily remained still, to observe the spectacle. This dead man, I said to myself, has perhaps friends, and he is lying there abandoned by all but his dog! What a lesson nature teaches us by means of an animal.' ... I looked on, unmoved, at battles which decided the future of nations. Tearless, I had given orders which brought death to thousands. Yet here I was stirred, profoundly stirred, stirred to tears. And by what? By the grief of one dog.

It is said that the scene of the dog's loyalty haunted Napoleon until his own death. Perhaps a fitting sentiment for a man that found a purpose in the quest for power but really needed the undying loyalty of a friend.

Travels with Charley

Another variation on the underdog theme is a person that stands up for the little guy. Writer John Steinbeck (1902-1968) was born and raised on modest middle class means in his beloved Salinas Valley, California. These fertile valleys are the backdrops of many of his best-known stories. Yet, the irony of such a bountiful area is that while on one hand its yield helps feed parts of a country and at the same time those that do the labor of picking crops survive in a paltry manner. The tension between the haves and have nots is sharply felt by the Depression area survivors in Steinbeck's life and his books.

"I'll be ever'where -- wherever you look. Wherever they's a fight so hungry people can eat, I'll be there. Wherever they's a cop beatin' up a guy, I'll be there. . . . An' when our folks eat the stuff they raise an' live in the houses they build -- why, I'll be there." *The Grapes of Wrath*

Steinbeck's introduction to becoming a writer of social protest, and advocate role for the underdog was in his youth. His mother, a former teacher, introduced her son to reading, which he did in a voracious way throughout his life. He would also work high school summer vacations alongside those who made a living literally from hand to mouth, many of whom were migrant Oklahomans picking crops to eke out a living. Steinbeck was left with a clearer view of an America that overlooked the disenfranchised and hurting people of the Depression era. Throughout his career as a writer, he worked to change that oversight in books such as *Grapes of Wrath*, *The Flat Tortilla*, and *Of Mice and Men*.

Steinbeck the writer would continue to sell books long after his death, some 700,000 copies each year. New York Times writer Terry Teachout argues if sales equal success, the posthumous career of John Steinbeck is one of the most successful in modern American literature. Yet, before his fame, Steinbeck was an underdog writer that no publishers wanted. A huge mystery to him was how he finally got his break after what seemed like an endless period of rejection. Publishers that did take a chance on his early books found them to be commercial failures. Perhaps adding insult to injury was all his early publishers went bankrupt. Even when he was hugely successful, and awarded the Nobel Prize in 1962, he was deeply hurt by literary critics that thought such accolades belonged with younger writers of a different modern era.

Interpersonally, John Steinbeck was down to earth. He seemed to take real joy in interacting with the locals. It could be in garages, coffee shops, or by chance encounters that stirred up a spontaneous conversation. He wore sweatshirts and chinos. He drank jug red wine. His late-night meals included chili beans and tuna fish on crackers. The American reading public sensed in Steinbeck not only his essential compassion, but lack of snobbery. They seemed to resonate with an author that felt like one of them. He was a voice for ordinary American people, places, and things.

But at the age of fifty-eight, it came to him with a shock that for more than twenty years he had not seen the country he had long written about. So, began the thrust for the book, *Travels with Charley*, a sojourn across America. Charley is a French poodle, Steinbeck's dog and road trip buddy. Charley and Steinbeck set off on what seems like an epic adventure. Something akin to Don Quixote, giving chase to one more round of windmills. In fact, he names his travel camper after Don Quixote's horse, Rocinante, the "horse that used to be ordinary." An "old nag" transformed to the "foremost" steed. A type of metamorphosis that we would expect from someone pulling for the underdog. Charley takes up a supporting player role in the spirit of Sancho Panza. Sancho is the paragon of a realistic and practical approach, the counterbalance to the idealistic and sometimes delusional Don Quixote. Adding to the background of the storyline is Steinbeck was extremely depressed during this time, in bad health, and was discouraged by family and friends from making the trip. In a way he was trying to recapture his youth, the spirit of the knight-errant.

In his travelogue, Steinbeck finds much to praise about the America he sees, but he does not avoid addressing its shortcomings. There is a lot that Steinbeck mourns for along the way. In one striking example, Steinbeck drove to New Orleans' Ninth Ward, a racially diverse and poverty-stricken area, rife with tension in 1960. There he witnessed the angry protests by white mothers outside a recently integrated public school. The encounter depressed him. Steinbeck turns around heading back north and, in his heart, he knows the journey is over. Steinbeck finds himself back home in New York where, ironically, he realizes that he is lost. He must ask for directions. As he spent a good deal of his journey lost, it is likely being lost is a metaphor for how much America has changed in Steinbeck's eyes. He does not recognize it anymore.

I think on some level Steinbeck hoped to find a different America, a better one. One that reflected the changes he advocated for throughout his career. But what he finds instead is the next round of uncertain futures and troubling issues to be addressed. That can be a disheartening realization when one has spent their entire life fighting for the little guy. It can leave a person thinking their efforts did not matter because disturbing social issues have not been eradicated. All of this when Steinbeck is at that place in life when many of us do a life review. What have my efforts really yielded? Curiously, at the end of the tale of Don Quixote he finally arrives home to La Manchua. He decides to set out on another quest, but he is too badly beaten and battered. In his despair, Don Quixote renounces his chivalric ideals bringing on a fever from which he dies. In mythic terms, so dies the knight-errant. Perhaps this tale embedded within Steinbeck's mind resonates a little too closely with his own predicament.

The story that stands out to me though is Steinbeck drives through the Mojave Desert. Charley is thirsty and badly in need of a drink of water.

Steinbeck pulls over in a gully and is startled by a pair of curious coyotes fifty yards away. At first, he sees the coyotes as a chicken stealing menace and readies his rifle to shoot them.

> "And then the coyote sat down like a dog and its right rear paw came up to scratch   the right shoulder."

Shaking off "ancient conditioning" he experiences a newfound empathy, seeing the coyotes in a new way.

> "Now I have taken responsibility for two live and healthy coyotes…"
> "In the   delicate world of relationships, we are tied together for all time. I opened two cans   of dog food and left them as a votive."

He sits a bit and reflects on the resiliency of desert life:

> "I find most interesting the conspiracy of life in the desert to circumvent the death rays of the all-conquering sun…" "The beaten earth appears defeated and dead, but it only appears so. A vast and inventive organization of living matter survives by seeming to have lost."

Perhaps Steinbeck sees himself in that arid landscape as well. At first glance defeated, "but it only appears so." There is a hopeful note in that story.

"These trained and tested fragments of life might well be the last hope of life against   non-life..." "The   desert   has   mothered magic things before this."

 Steinbeck may realize in these moments his efforts were not in vain. He is just passing the torch to the next generation. Where the magic of life and championing the underdog will continue.

There have been some subsequent questions about the validity of Steinbeck's actual journey, how much was undertaken and the legitimacy of those he meets. Were these fictionalized accounts? Even if they are, I am not troubled by these notions. Perhaps this is a tale of art imitating life. Steinbeck's travelogue with Charley is the type of mythological journey enhanced by having a dog along for the ride.

Section III: Healers

Dating back to antiquity there is the presence of animals in rituals of health and healing. In ancient Greece, dogs were utilized in the Temple of Apollo. In what may seem like a type of spa treatment, patients were attended by canines that would lick the sick or ailing body parts. The thought being dogs would remove the cause of sickness through their tender ministrations. A similar theme involved St Roch the patron saint of dogs. It was believed that this medieval man was healed of the plague by the same canine cure. Among some Native American tribes are stories about the various important role's dogs play within the community. While canines assumed the practical task of carrying packs, an essential function for a nomadic people accustomed to moving with the seasons, it was also believed that these animal companions possessed a magical nature. Dogs were imbued with the ability to portend good/bad omens and see into the spirit world where humans could not. However, most remarkable was their ability to absorb and carry the pain, sorrow, and physical troubles of tribe members. The story goes that a dog would bear these ailments to make a human being's load lighter.

Psychoanalyst Sigmund Freud's Chow dogs were omnipresent in his consulting room. It was suggested that the dogs were originally in the office for Freud's benefit, to help him feel more relaxed. He felt a good bit of anxiety and the burden of having people stare at him throughout the day. Not a small thing for a man that had over thirty cancer operations on his jaw. Later Freud recognized that his patients also seemed to value the dogs' presence.

Child psychologist, Boris Levinson, however, is credited as the father of modern animal assisted therapy (AAT). AAT utilizes the presence of animals, especially dogs, in the therapy office and beyond. Many of the inhibited and uncommunicative children in Levinson's clinical practice responded positively to his dog Jingles.

My job in this book is primarily as the narrator of other men's stories. The role also draws to mind my own experience with canine companions. Like the lives of the men found in this section I have also been raised to a better place for having known my animal friends. I have spent many years thinking about why dogs are successful change agents in men's lives. That is, they encourage us to think, act, and feel in ways previously thought impossible. This is not some 180-degree shift in our nature which my experience as a psychologist tells me does not exist for anyone. Rather, in the company of our animal companions we take small and often labored steps to better ways of living.

Even this type of inspired change seems astounding to me especially when compared to other human helpers that have gone beforehand. These include family and friends with good intentions, or those possessing advanced degrees in social sciences, or having acquired a specialized set of listening skills. The title of this section is "Healers;" a phrase which could be the appropriate way to refer to both man and dog.

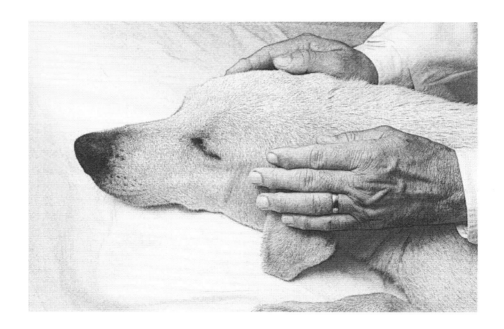

Saint Roch

The truth I do not stretch or shove When I state that the
dog is full of love.
The Dog, Ogden Nash

The man who later becomes known as St. Roch has a personal history clouded with legend. He was born of a noble house in France and is believed to have lived from around 1295 to 1327. His father was the governor of the city Montpellier. The young Roch was deeply spiritual even as a boy, fasting twice a week. On his father's deathbed he asked Roch to take the family's wealth and live a charitable life, attending to the sick and poor. Roch fulfilled his pledge. He left the governmental roles to his uncle's care and donned the uniform of a Franciscan mendicant pilgrim. Mendicant pilgrims (or 'begging friars') take a vow of poverty and focus their time and energy on serving the sick and poor. They can usually be identified in this Western timeframe as wearing a grey habit. The life of a mendicant is not an easy one, their survival was dependent upon the good will of others to feed and house them. In many cases, necessity prompted them to be perpetually on the road. The ascetic way of life takes Roch across France, Spain, and Italy. On his travels tending the sick, Roch also contracted the plague. One version of the story goes he realized his time had come so he retreated to the forest to face his end. As he lay dying, a mysterious dog appeared. The dog began to lick his wounds slowly healing the illness. Each day the dog would continue his gentle care while also showing up with a loaf of bread in his mouth. Over time, Roch recovered. Roch and the dog continued their journey together.

On the return home to France, Roch was mistaken as a spy amid an intense civil war. It is said that Roch and his dog were both imprisoned for five years where they tended to fellow prisoners until the saint's death in 1327.

Saint Roch is rightfully represented in statuary and pictorial form as a pilgrim accompanied by a dog. Roch is sometimes depicted as wearing a traveler's hat and carrying a staff representing his wandering lifestyle. One version of the artistic depictions has the dog carrying a loaf of bread in its mouth. Almost all versions include Roch pointing to his thigh showing where the dog healed him of the plague.

St Roch is the patron saint of several causes including those falsely accused, and those in need of relief from epidemics. It may not be a coincidence that he also champions the cause of dogs and bachelors. The latter two being deeply connected not only in the story of Roch but finding its way to the present day. Roch's death is commemorated on August 16th.

One may wonder why a saint from the Middle Ages is still venerated today. Given that modern medicine appears late on the scene, illness, epidemic, and death are never far away. The story of St Roch is recycled in a time of need both in Europe and the United States. One example is taken from a 19th century yellow fever and cholera epidemic that occurred in New Orleans, Louisiana. The reverend Peter Thevis vowed that if his congregation was spared from the outbreak, he would build a chapel to honor St. Roch. Having those prayers answered, the St. Roch Chapel and accompanying cemetery were founded in 1874. Both are sites that have been popular pilgrimage spots for more than 150 years. In the small chapel there are various 'ex-votos,' tokens of thanks for healing that include candles, small figures, and notes inscribed on bricks. There are also relics of a different kind that include glass eyes, dental plates, crutches, an old prosthetic leg, and a decayed polio brace. These are relics of those that left their burdens behind.

One might wonder if Roch is honored at the chapel then where is the dog? Visitors are not to be disappointed as a ghost of a dog is often seen wandering through the Cemetery. However, there is no mention whether or not he carries a loaf of bread or is likely to lick your sores.

His Damn Dog

Dogs love their friends and bite their enemies quite unlike people, who are incapable of pure love and always have to mix love and hate in their object-relations.
Sigmund Freud

If you allow yourself to free associate about psychoanalyst Sigmund Freud, the first thing that comes to mind may not be "a devoted dog lover." Yet, his bond with his Chow dogs named Joffie and Luna would make up a significant part of his later years.

In Freud's middle age he published a seminal paper titled, "Mourning and Melancholia." It discusses the differences between someone that is grieving versus that of being depressed. In many cases there can be a fine line between the two. Freud offered that with depression you personally feel poorer, levels of self-esteem plunging. With grief on the other hand, the world feels poorer for the absence of a loved one. Freud's perspectives on these matters were presented in 1917 but they have remained for one hundred years as a description of what grieving looks like. Freud would personally revisit his earlier work on mourning and melancholia after many painful losses in his own life.

In 1923, at the age of 62, Freud was diagnosed with cancer of the jaw. Over the next 16 years he endured 30 operations eventually making use of a prosthetic jaw. Initially his doctor decided to spare Freud the verdict fearing the already taxed man would lose hope. But after the truth was revealed, Freud inquired of his doctor if he would help him "disappear from this world with decency" if the suffering was too great.

The cancer diagnosis was just another in the line of losses and transitions that had already occurred, with more to come. Earlier in 1920, Freud had seen the passing of his closest daughter, Sophie. She died in an influenza epidemic. Shortly afterward, his four-year old grandson Heinz passed away due to tuberculosis. The relationship with his remaining daughter, Anna, also began transforming. Freud relied heavily upon her for many years, but Anna was now becoming her own person. The result was that Freud felt alone.

Professionally the science of psychoanalysis that he loved and worked so hard to create, was growing but that also meant those in his inner circle began forming opinions of their own. This was something Freud could not tolerate leading to estrangement from a number of friends, colleagues, and series of heir apparents.

Freud also had to flee his home in Vienna because of mounting political issues that led to World War II. Four of Freud's five sisters and his maternal grandmother would later perish in concentration camps. At one point Freud relied on friends and colleagues for financial support. One of those was Princess Marie Bonaparte, a descendant of Lucien Bonaparte, brother of the Emperor Napoleon of France. Besides psychoanalysis, Freud and Marie shared in common the love of dogs. It is in a letter to Marie that Freud outlines his position about dog's steadfast nature and their ability to provide a type of pure love free of ambivalent feelings. Something so unaccustomed in our relationships with humans.

These notes are striking in the context of Freud's new life. After Freud's Vienna consulting room was replicated in faithful detail in the new family home located in North London, things were not the same, in fact, life circumstances continued to evolve. Amid these various losses, Freud confided to a friend that he believed himself incapable of loving again. It was in this part of his life when he would eventually find some relief in the company of his dogs.

For many years already, Freud had had a special connection with animals, especially dogs. He and his daughter, Anna, wrote birthday rhymes and poetry to one another in the guise of their German shepherd. But in the midst of mounting losses, his animal companions took on a new, significant role. It is noted that Freud was often photographed traveling with one of his Chows. In fact, he became inseparable from them. Freud, who also now wore a prosthetic jaw as the result of cancer, even made good use of his dog's canine teeth on his behalf at meals. He allowed his dog to masticate his meat so he could eat it.

Joffie was also omnipresent in his consultation room. It has been suggested the initial presence of his dog was not so much for his patients but was rather a steadying influence on him. Apparently, Freud's canine co-therapist also had her own couch and would rise from it when time for the session was up. There was no need for a clock. Joffie also had a habit of screening Freud's would-be patients. The word was that she would meet a prospective patient at the door and only if she approved would the person gain entrance. One patient who underwent this vetting process stated that he was not so worried about Freud liking him, but he felt a real pressure to win over "his damn dog."

Grief and loss can accentuate the need we also have to find a friend. Especially if we feel compelled to pull away from others and withdraw into ourselves. What is unique about our canine companions is their silent presence has a steadfast therapeutic effect. They make the world seem a bit brighter even if it feels poorer for the loss of a loved one.

Animal assisted therapy

Can a pet actually be our own personal therapist? Child psychologist Boris Levinson thought something along those lines and is credited as being the father of what is referred to as animal assisted therapy (AAT). AAT involves when an animal, usually a dog, plays a special type of role, as a sort of co-therapist. They can assume this job in a traditional counseling setting or ones that move the work into the great outdoors. The animal's role can vary but most approaches emphasize how dogs help clients build rapport with a therapist. This is sometimes referred to as the dog being a 'social lubricant' helping anxious or traumatized clients feel more at ease in what can be a stressful situation - expressing and exploring one's pain. The hope is the bond between the client and dog will eventually transfer to that of the therapist setting the stage for successful treatment. For some, it is much easier to bond with a dog if human beings have been a source of severe let downs.

The work of an AAT can also sometimes occur outside a therapist's office. AAT is used with children in adjudicated settings, where a boy or girl may learn about dog training to help hard to adopt shelter dogs find a forever home. Recent research suggests children also benefit by participating in such programs. Many shows marked improvements in terms of emotional intelligence, empathy, and decreases in the behaviors that originally got them in trouble with the law. The progression is based on experiencing a bond with a dog that is unique, one never previously encountered that feels supportive and caring.

For adults, AAT can provide a steady connection for those returning from military duty in war torn areas suffering from post-traumatic stress disorder. The condition is characterized by flashbacks to traumatic events such as friends, colleagues, and the innocent being harmed. Those with PTSD have an inability to relax, having a startle response that perceives unexpected and familiar sounds as potentially life threatening. In this case, the backfire of a car may sound too much like the firing of a gun. In this context dogs are not only a source of comfort in the moments when flashbacks occur, but they learn the physical cues that indicate their human friend is beginning to have a painful memory and intervene. This may include taking steps to draw the person's attention back to the present by placing a gentle paw on their friend. The bond literally sets the stage for the body and mind healing from the conditioned responses of overwhelming danger.

If we turn back the clock, we can see the origins of AAT taking shape in Levinson's office. Many of the children in Levinson's clinical practice who were withdrawn and uncommunicative would interact more freely with his dog Jingles. He made this breakthrough by chance one day leaving Jingles with a child client as he stepped out of the office. Upon his return, Levinson noted that the once inhibited child now interacted enthusiastically with his dog, setting the stage for counseling to begin. Even with this breakthrough, Boris Levinson's journey to make animal-assisted therapy legitimate in the eyes of the professional world was not an easy one. In the 1960s, he argued for the importance of human-animal interaction to his colleagues at the American Psychological Association convention, only to be nearly laughed out of the meeting.

Today, we have a better idea of the potential impact that animal companions have in our lives in terms of health and well-being. Studies over the years point to how dogs help us feel better especially if we are alone, with limited social support. That type of connection can also make the difference for those recovering from surgery. In one of the first studies to document the healthy impact of animal companions in our lives, patients recovering from heart surgery had significantly higher survival rates if they had a dog. Since then, studies have extended the healing effect of dogs in many directions. But even those in less dire circumstances with a well-established social network of family and friends benefit from the bond. That speaks to something very special occurring when we interact with our four-legged friends. One of the most quintessential of all human needs is to have another present in our lives, a type of companion on life's journey. This includes having someone be there across a wide array of ups and downs.

Section IV: Adventurers

There are two types of adventurers. One version ventures off into unknown physical realms – this is the undiscovered country that can include oceans, mountains, and even outer space. The journey is in part to push the envelope in the words of one famous space captain, "...where no man has gone before." But it also involves far more than just being the first to plant a flag. The adventurer is changed in some fundamental way by the expedition. It could result in new knowledge like how 19th century explorers helped discover better understanding of the natural world. Or how an astronaut, when viewing the Earth from space, makes note that there are no naturally occurring boundaries between countries even if ideologies keep them all but separated.

The second type of adventurer has a similar goal of journeying into unknown places. But in these instances, the sojourns are ones to the inner world of thoughts and feelings. The purpose of the trek is to look for previously unrecognized insights. Carl Jung and Sigmund Freud were special types of explorers of the innermost realm whose adventures allowed for authoritatively commenting upon new psychological understandings.

Whether the journey is to the external or internal worlds, you do not have to be among the first or most expert to achieve similar effects as the explorers mentioned above. Everyday people like you and me sometimes intentionally and sometimes inadvertently set foot on a path leading us to our own version of *terra nova*, the new land. It involves seeing a vista that draws us into the moment or coming to a better realization of one's own life story. In either case, all adventurers follow what mythologist Joseph Campbell referred to as a hero's journey.

Campbell makes note that the would-be hero leaves the safe surroundings of home. Sometimes there is a mysterious sign like the appearance of a golden stag that draws the adventurer unwittingly deep into an unknown wood. In other cases, there are grail chasers that have a specific quest in mind. One of the exciting parts of the journey is even with the best map in hand no one knows the real twists and turns that lie ahead. The hero is slowly transformed by each trial that accompanies the expedition. The trip builds to a crescendo culminating by entering the pivotal place referred to by Campbell as a 'personal labyrinth.' You may remember stories of how at the center of such places there lies a monster or a mystery that puts us into direct contact with our deepest hopes, fears, or unresolved issues. It is by facing these elements that we are changed into different people, literally turning us into a hero within our own personal narrative. The hero can find new insights about the connectedness of all living beings. Or, on another type of trek discovering how all the chapters of one's life fit together in a more peaceful and meaningful way.

If facing a labyrinth where the most ferocious monsters and interpersonal conflicts reside sounds like a daunting task, the good news is we rarely face it alone. There can be a friend, mentor, or a guide that accompanies us to the places we have yet to master. For some, a dog goes with us every step of the way.

The dog is uniquely prepared for the role of companion on the hero's journey. Dogs as seen through the lens of Campbell's hero's journey can sometimes assume the role of a 'psychopomp.' That is, dogs become a guide for us when venturing in unknown places. Dogs are uniquely qualified for this role. A canine companion reminds us that we need to face our excursion as whole persons with all our potential assets present. It is disconcerting to discover we have set off on our most challenging expedition with missing resources. We may remember to bring a tent and flashlight, but other needed elements may be missing or only to be found later on the path. Sometimes what is learned along the way is that we have some underdeveloped parts of our psyche, or we need to boost our skills set if we are to be successfully climbing the mountain, facing the Minotaur, or really loving someone in a way not previously known. The required stretch can include certain emotions or behaviors we have previously labelled as off-limits though now they are necessary ones to complete the trek.

A canine companion is outfitted for the journey through his/her unique DNA. The dog is the descendent of the wolf, carrying a hint of a wildness into every adventure. Given what we will encounter in the new world is unknown, our dog is a reminder to stay in touch with our own hardwired instincts. When we walk alongside a dog, we are promoted to acknowledge a sense of wildness is not only okay but a benefit if we know how to keep it focused.

Each of the men we encounter in this section found the company of a dog beneficial if not essential on the journey. Each was changed in some way. In some instances, it was prolonged contact, in other instances a canine companion made a life changing impact in just a few moments. A dog's presence is a grounding one for those that step into unknown worlds.

.

Horatio and Bud

In May of 1903, Dr. Horatio Nelson Jackson set off from San Francisco to New York in a 20-horse powered automobile. He named the car "the Vermont" after his home state. Jackson was a novice driver still learning to be comfortable behind the wheel. So, he convinced a young mechanic named Sewall K. Crocker to accompany him. At the time, many believed that the automobile was a passing fade. The pair hoped to prove otherwise by being the first persons to cross the United States in the "horseless carriage." While Jackson was not the first to attempt this feat, he put his money where his mouth was by placing a fifty-dollar bet that the duo would succeed in less than 90 days. While Jackson seemed to possess a strong resolve, the journey was actually a spur of the moment decision. He had recently returned from Alaska investing in mining operations. He was having dinner and drinks in a San Francisco gentlemen's club when the conversation turned to the future of the motor car. Most seemed skeptical not just about the automobile's future but the possibility that anyone could make a transcontinental journey in one. All the nay seers seemed only to stoke Jackson's conviction and determination. Four days after the fateful night, Jackson had acquired his automobile and started the trip.

The nearly 3000-mile trip across the United States was fraught with unexpected problems that included frequent mechanical failure, running out of gasoline and oil. Another difficulty was wrong turns and inaccurate maps only added mileage to the trek, sometimes undoing the entire day's efforts. Nearly all the parts on the Vermont had to be replaced mid-journey. Blacksmiths in various towns were employed on several occasions to replace parts and put the car back together. It is important to recognize that at that time, there was not exactly a surplus of automobile dealerships for service or spare parts. Each had to be shipped by train to the destination, only adding more time to the journey. In one instance, a cowboy on horseback lassoed and then towed the car to a nearby ranch for repairs.

The driving expedition was also loud and bumpy. There were few roads that we would consider passable by today's standards. In fact, it has been estimated that only 150 miles of paved road existed throughout the entire United States at the time of the journey. The noise of the car also concealed the fact that the necessary equipment made a regular exit from the back of the car, where the backseat had been removed for storage. At one point, cooking equipment had fallen off the back, and at some point, Jackson's coat followed suit, containing most of the travelers' money. Jackson had to wire and rewire his wife several times for funds.

Throughout all the travel difficulties Jackson maintained an unbelievable optimism. He wrote heart-felt love letters to his wife that also convey that each bit of bad luck would surely be the last, leading only to smooth sailing for the rest of the journey. He found his resolve time and again enjoying the journey of a lifetime.

Jackson and Crocker obtained a Bulldog named Bud near Caldwell, Idaho. It turns out that Jackson had wanted a canine companion to join the expedition since leaving California. Jackson remarked that Bud was the only one of the trio in the car that did not use profanity when road hazards impeded the trip. As the word of the journey spread, the threesome became celebrities. The press came out regularly at scheduled stops taking pictures and conducting interviews. In the spirit of the modern-day paparazzi, newspapers offered a variety of eye-catching stories. They included scandalous rumors and daring speculation on how Bud was acquired. Was he found or stolen? But to clarify matters, Nelson, in a letter to his wife, explained how he bought Bud from a man for $15. While Bud was a good traveler, it turned out that the dusty roads bothered his eyes a great deal. This was only made worse by the fact that the Vermont did not possess a roof or windshield. Jackson fitted Bud with a pair of driving goggles. Bud the dog was celebrated for his fashion-forward sense of style, wearing new eye wear over the remainder of the long journey.

After 63 days, 12 hours, and 30 minutes the driving team that would have been the envy of any racing team at Lemans, arrived in New York completing the nearly 3000 mile journey across the North American continent. From there, Jackson almost made it to his house in Vermont before the last part on the automobile that had not been repaired finally broke.

As for Jackson in his later years, he served in World War I though into his 40's at the time and was one of the founders of the American Legion. He was a successful businessman and ran for Governor of Vermont twice. Jackson would gladly tell anyone willing to listen of the journey across America. He was even ticketed once for exceeding the 6-mph speed limit in Burlington. And by all accounts, Bud lived a long happy life passing away at age 19.

For many of us driving is far more than a way of getting from point A to B. Instead, it takes the form of a much-beloved pastime. It is the way to extend the weekend through taking a Sunday drive. It also displays our individuality through the choice of make and model. There are of course other ways to show who we are like the fuzzy dice hanging from the rearview mirror or a bumper sticker spouting our views on various issues for any passerby to read. At the heart of the journey across a continent was the sense of individual freedom to go wherever and whenever one pleased. Arguably something that takes on a universal appeal – the traveler and adventurer willing to make the journey for its own sake. And all the adversity Horatio, Crocker, and Bud encountered was a foreshadowing of the traveling family vacation replete with difficulties at every twist and turn. Ones that in hindsight only add to the sense of nostalgia we experience by way of the horseless carriage.

When we take a drive there does not even have to be a fixed destination. But on extended road trips the journey is not complete without a friend to ride along. Some of us are fortunate enough to call a dog our sidekick as we motor down life's highway.

The Last Explorer

Imagine standing on top of the world, literally. Or, for that matter, the bottom of it. In terms of longitude and latitude it is the only place on the globe that only needs one coordinate: 90 N degrees or -90 S degrees respectively, where all lines of longitude running north and south converge at one spot. The North and South Poles. In the early part of the 20th century there was a race for the poles. Who would be the first to reach it, fly over it, and map it on behalf of the Royal Geographic Society?

One way to couch the events' importance was that of scientific interest. This was Terra Nova, a new and unfamiliar land waiting for the outer limits of human exploration to occur. New land to see and maps to be drawn. Another view would be that the race to the poles was a sporting event on a grand scale in which various nations competed to see who could arrive first, laying claim based upon who planted the first flag.

But even in those terms, this was no leisure Sunday afternoon sport event, replete with brunch and comfortable chairs to rest upon after minimally exerting oneself. The race to the poles were events that held real dangers-life and death consequences where some did not return, and others were never found.

As a boy I remember reading about polar adventures. It felt like a way to vicariously learn about testing oneself against oneself in the guise of my personal Terra Nova. Adventuring tests what you are made of. While I did not commit to memory all the facts and figures about the various 'firsts,' regarding the race for the poles, what did stay with me was the potential thrill of exploration. Even if it were on a miniscule scale by comparison, it became synonymous with really living. That sense stays with me even to the present day. Looking back over my life at beyond middle age, I think how the concept of exploring guided me in moments of big decisions. Moving to an unknown part of the country in my 20's to pursue training for a career that seemed impossible to achieve. Or, on the domestic side of things, telling a woman that I loved her. Even, entering the world of parenthood gazing at my son for the first time. I imagined what expeditions lay ahead on our life's journey together. All adventures to me. All things that not only stretched my sense of who I am but made life worth living. All these things made possible in part because I read about explorers searching for parts unknown that include the inner reaches of one's own heart and mind.

One of the reasons the person of discussion in this chapter made it to the fore in my personal estimation was he was an explorer with a dog. I think there is something ancient and archetypal about this combination, speaking to the deepest recesses of the imagination. For me, animal companions become both a sidekick and a safe base camp in various life adventures. Perhaps, they are for you as well...

To begin at the ending, on April 20th, 1931, famed polar explorer Admiral Richard E. Byrd was preparing to give a lecture in Springfield IL. He had recently returned from his well-celebrated expedition to Antarctica. As was the custom in the times, explorers entered the lecture circuit when returning from their adventures. It was a way to involve the public. And it was also a practical way to offset expenses accrued from traveling to remote places a long time before there were cut-rate internet fares. This evening though, Admiral Byrd received a disturbing message regarding his dog Igloo. Igloo had taken ill over the past several days. He had been examined by at least three veterinarians in trying to assist with the dog's severe indigestion. It was later discovered that the short haired terrier who had become Admiral Byrd constant companion over their six years together had likely ingested rat poison. When the news about Igloo's condition reached Byrd, he immediately cancelled the night's lecture and took a train and then hired a private plane to fly him back home to Boston. Unfortunately, Igloo's condition was not successfully treated, and he passed away before Byrd reached him.

The story of this unlikely friendship between one who was widely considered the last great explorer and a homeless wire-haired terrier puppy seems the stuff of legend. But as we will see, it is not only real, but epitomizes the bond highlighted in this book.

Richard Byrd knew from an early age that he was drawn to the adventure. In fact, at 14 years-old he was given a chance to travel around the world for a year enroute to staying with an aunt and uncle in the Philippines. Byrd later entered the navy and with the onset of World War I reenlisted as a pilot. In keeping with his customary charm and ability to negotiate, he had to persuade the examining doctor at his physical to give him a chance to become an aviator. Not an easy task for someone that suffered severe leg fractures on three occasions. And walked with a limp.   Byrd would later not only become a successful flyer, but invented instruments to help aviators gauge how far a storm set them off course (long before the invention of radar). But it was not well known at the time that flying made Byrd airsick. Perhaps not the thing to reveal to the public hungry for stories of new adventures, nor financiers backing the expeditions. The way he solved this problem was to assume the role of navigator charting the course while relying upon a trusted friend to steer the plane. The approach was the solution aiding the daring attempts and eventual success of flying over both the North and South Poles.

Byrd met Igloo by chance. He was preparing for the 1926 voyage to the Arctic pole when he was contacted by Maris Boggs. She was a vague acquaintance that he had met a month or so earlier. She offered him a dog for his journey. One she had found cold and shivering on the streets of Washington, D.C. At first Byrd refused, but for some reason he eventually relented. Maris delivered Igloo in a wicker basket accompanied by a dog-sized sweater to keep the little puppy warm on the trip. It would not be the last time someone thought to outfit Igloo for an adventure to the pole.

With much difficulty, May 9, 1926, Byrd and pilot Floyd Bennett attempted a flight over the North Pole. They were flying a tri-motor monoplane. Byrd knew that it was commonplace for engines to stall in such cold weather. So, he figured if two went out he would have at least one to power the plane home. The flight lasted 15 hours and 57 minutes covering a distance of 1,535 miles. Igloo was not on board, but was on the long journey to and from the Arctic. Byrd became a national sensation. He was prompted to the rank of Admiral and both he and his pilot were awarded the Medal of Honor.

Not one to rest on his laurels, Byrd in 1928, began his first expedition to the other end of the world, the South Pole. The North Pole was a harsh environment. A floating drifting landmark located within the Arctic Ocean and buried under ice. While the South Pole, was a landmass covered with ice, hosting much harsher weather conditions including endless sub-zero temperatures. The weather would pose even more dangerous challenges to the crew, the planes, and to Igloo. To help Igloo stay warm the tailor onboard the ship made special parkas and boots to help the little dog brave the elements.

Both Byrd and Igloo are pictured above in their cold weather gear.

One of the common problems besides engine failure was ridding the plane of all non-essential weight to gain enough altitude. Byrd and the crew emptied gas tanks, and emergency supplies. Any unforeseen crash would lead to certain death. On November 28, 1929, the first flight over the South Pole occurred lasting 18 hours, 41 minutes.

Besides having a natural charisma, Byrd was seen as a bit of a showman for his time. Byrd actively cultivated relationships with influential individuals, ones that could help support his expeditions. The A list included Henry Ford, and his son Edsel Ford, owners of the Ford Motor company. As a token of his gratitude, Byrd utilized an early version of naming rights. He christened geographic features in the Antarctic after his supporters and in one case the name of the plane that flew over the North Pole after Ford's daughter. Knowing the South Pole trip would also be of keen interest to the public, their trip was also documented through photographs and film.

Upon the successful mission over the South Pole, he was given another hero's welcome back home. He met with President Hoover who awarded him a medal after the successful Antarctica campaign. Igloo not to be out done, he was also presented with a medal by the Tail Waggers Club, a society devoted to animal rights. Byrd also received a ticker tape parade upon his return to New York. Of course, the little wire terrier was sitting on the top of the back seat of the open convertible as they drove past the cheering crowd.

After Igloo's passing, Admiral Byrd would eventually return to the base camp known as Little America nestled in the cold windswept land of Antarctica. The place where he and Igloo weathered the storms together preparing for the flight over the South Pole. Upon arrival Byrd found one of Igloo's favorite toys. A ball with a cat face painted on it. A toy Igloo loved to have the crew of the expedition hide for him at least a few times a day. I think how the warmth of that memory must have kept Richard Byrd company on the long winter days and nights without his friend.

Igloo is buried outside of Boston in Dedham, Massachusetts. The gravestone is appropriately carved in the shape of an iceberg with the inscription taken directly from Byrd: "He was more than a friend."

I dream of that dog yet

Arthur Treadwell Walden was born in the Midwest of the United States in 1871. He was the son of a well-known Episcopal minister. Walden spent much of his formative years in Minnesota including being educated at the Chattuck Military School. When his father took a new position in Boston, Author did not find the urban surroundings to his liking. He subsequently moved to the family's vacation home in Tamworth, New Hampshire. It was that move that set Walden's fate in motion. His tale is one of an adventurer whose life is deeply impacted by dogs.

The young Walden familiarized himself with his New Hampshire surroundings and was hired by Kate Sleeper, the daughter of a wealthy Boston newspaperman, who owned the 100-acre Wonalancet farm in New Hampshire. Arthur worked as the farm manager before he left for the Klondike Gold Rush in Alaska. Walden was 24 years-old when he went on the Alaskan adventure. He worked at several different types of occupations including as a prospector, logger, and river pilot. But the vocation that would set the stage for his life's work was hauling freight by dogsled also known then as "dog punching," a type of cowboy with a dog pulled sled. After six years in the Northern territory, Walden returned to Wonalancet Farm where he married Kate in 1902. Together they ran an inn on the Wonalancet Farm. The remote picturesque area also allowed Walden's to pursue his real passion of establishing a new line of sled dogs.

On January 17, 1917, a litter of puppies was born to Walden's Greenland Husky, Ningo. Ningo was the granddaughter of polar explorer Admiral Robert Peary's lead dog from his 1909 Arctic expedition; a dog named Polaris. The pups were sired by a farm stray named Kim, a large mixed breed mastiff dog. In the litter there were three large pups that Walden's wife named Rikki, Tikki, and Tavi, after the mongoose tale written by Rudyard Kipling in the Jungle Book. One of the pups who at first seemed overshadowed by his siblings would eventually go on to dog immortality. He was renamed Chinook after an Eskimo dog Walden worked with during his Alaska exploits. He not only became Walden's constant companion, but Chinook made a name for himself setting dogsled records and helping popularize the sport in America. His name became synonymous with a new breed of sled dog line – the Chinook.

Both Walden and Chinook seemed gifted at public relations. Walden knew how to draw the public in and once there, the large, gentle giant Chinook won their hearts. Chinook's friendly, intelligent nature made him a local celebrity, including the children who wanted to play. For a dog that was so big and full of energy Chinook easily engaged both young and old in a calm way. Chinook could also turn into a couch potato after a long day romping in the snow. He was a family pet that could pull heavy loads and also sit by the fire at the end of the day. The perfect scenario for a close encounter with the amazing dog.

The 'Chinooks' became a tourist attraction at Wonalancet Farm. Visitors to the farm wanted to see the New England Sled Dogs Club's best and brightest. Rumor was that the team was so well-trained Walden would send Chinook and the other members out with an unmanned sled. Walden would then shout commands by megaphone from the porch of his home.

In 1922, Walden helped promote the first sled race in New Hampshire. With the local paper to sponsor the event, the first Eastern International Dog Derby was held. The race was 123 miles. Through Walden and Chinook's efforts the New England Sled Dog Club was founded in 1924. It is the oldest continuous U.S. sled dog club. It has held dog sled races since its founding except for a brief span during World War II. The sled driving pair began attracting attention beyond his New Hampshire farm. In 1927, Walden was invited by explorer Admiral Richard E. Byrd to join his latest expedition. to the sub-zero temperatures of the Antarctic. Walden agreed with the stipulation that no dogs would be sacrificed to save supplies, a miserable custom of the day.

Walden took Chinook to the coldest place on earth, even though he was now past his prime at eleven years old. Even with his advanced age Chinook was still the lead dog among his fifteen sons that also made the trip.

Walden's team had a significant presence among the other 100 dogs who would all work together hauling the 500 tons of supplies from Byrd's ship to the new Antarctic base named "Little America." Walden was 58 years-old.

Byrd wrote about Walden and Chinook commenting how both man and dog outshone their younger colleagues in terms of work ethic and resolve. Byrd wrote that when the going got rough Walden would place Chinook in a harness providing inspiration for the dog team:

> "...there was no doubting the fact that he was a great dog. ...Walden used him as kind of a "shock troop", throwing him into harness when the going turned very hard. Then the gallant heart of the old dog would rise above the years and pull with the glorious strength of a three-year-old."

On January 17th, 1929, Walden's team of dogs set a new daily record by moving 3,500 pounds of supplies in two trips from ship to base, a total distance of 32 miles. The night after the record was set Chinook woke Walden several times putting his paw on his shoulder. At the time Walden did not think much of this and patted his friend as a way of saying go back to sleep. It was not until later that Walden realized his trusty and determined companion was saying goodbye. Due to the Arctic dangers the sled team of dogs worked in pairs. Chinook not always harnessed would run alongside or sometimes behind the pack. Walden was careful not to overwork his aging friend and would only place him as the lead dog position when an inspired team effort was needed.

While it happened occasionally that Chinook arrived at the base after the team, on the following day after the record he did not return at all. The rest of the crew feared that he had fallen into a crevice. But Walden began putting the pieces of the puzzle together; the previous day Chinook was downed by three dogs that simultaneously challenged his leader role. It was the first time he was bested in such a contest. When Walden set out the next day Chinook ran behind the sled team and when he looked away, Walden never saw his companion again. Walden believed Chinook had said his goodbyes the previous night and then wandered into the Antarctic freeze of 30 below zero to pass away. Walden said later about the passing of his friend, "I dream of that dog yet. I can't get him out of my mind."

While Walden wanted to bury Chinook in his harness as a way of memorializing his friend, he never got the chance. But Walden did honor him by having a new highway back home in Wonalancet named after him. At first Walden's hometown suggested that the thoroughfare have Walden's name, but he insisted it should be given to his loyal friend instead. The Chinook Trail still bears his name today.

Even amid the celebration of Walden's return from the South Pole, the expedition left him deep in debt. The stock market crash of 1929 further decimated the family's assets. A questionable financial transition also occurred in his absence that led to a former partner taking control of the farm. Walden's wife also had developed senility while he was away, and it is suggested by some the new owners exploited the situation. Making matters worse, they also claimed the rights to his kennel.

Never being one to stay down for long, Walden was able to acquire puppies of the Chinook lineage elsewhere from a friend. This enabled him to continue the breeding at relocated kennels. In his remaining years, Walden continued to write books, ones based on his sled adventures.

He also helped at sporting events and officiated sled races. Walden's wanderlust subdued upon return from the Byrd Expedition. One of the chief factors was his devotion to the care of his wife. He died in 1947 much in the heroic manner of how he lived, saving his wife from a house fire.

It would have been even more of a tragedy if the Walden story ended there. Instead, in 2009 New Hampshire made the official state dog the Chinook. A breed that nearly disappeared in the 1960s, with only 11 breedable dogs. Today there are more than 1,200 Chinooks in America and The American Kennel Club recognized the breed in 2012. Two years later the Chinook competed for the first time at the Westminster Kennel Club Dog Show. Both Author Walden and Chinook would have been proud.

The First Modern Man

Within Homer's twenty-eight-hundred-year-old work, The Odyssey, we find an unlikely action hero, at least by today's standards. Odysseus is more of a homebody. While he does have adventures in a far-off land, he would prefer being close to his wife Penelope, their son, and of course, his dog Argos. He is also known more for his brains than his brawn. When in a jam he comes up with solutions that are outside of the box. On one occasion he tied himself to the mast of his ship and stuffed beeswax in his ears to muffle the seductive call of sirens trying to lure him to a deadly reef. On another, he designed a giant hollowed out wooden horse to sneak his men into an impregnable city. He spent ten years fighting the Trojan War and another ten years trying to get back to his family in Ithaca. His clever nature and family's memory are what sustained him throughout. Odysseus left on what was supposed to be more of a three-hour cruise that unexpectedly turned into a twenty-year odyssey. Over the course of the journey, he and his crew go through a series of adventures on their complicated trip back home.

But having traversed much, Odysseus finally finds himself at the journey's end with one more problem to solve: dealing with the many suitors believing him dead and seeking the hand of his wife and the riches of his kingdom. So, keeping with Odysseus' signature style of coming up with a clever way out of a dilemma, he disguises himself as a beggar with the help of the goddess Athena. He is so well concealed, not even Penelope recognizes him. However, his faithful dog Argos knows him at the first glance. Argos has awaited his master's return for many years in less-than-ideal conditions.

> Now with his master gone he lay there, castaway, on plies of dung from mules and cattle ...Infested with ticks, half-dead from neglect, here he lay the hound, old Argos. But the moment he sensed Odysseus standing by he thumped his tail, nuzzling low, and his ears dropped, though he had no strength to drag himself an inch toward his master. Odysseus glanced to the side and flicked away a tear...

There is something exceptional about Odysseus' response. Not all tears are the same and this one suggests that Odysseus is moved in a very particular way. Maybe this comes from being overwhelmed with the absolute devotion and loyalty of an old friend. It may even have to do with Argos, like many canine companions, being a tangible sign to Odysseus that he is finally back home where he belongs. The origin of the tear may also have something to do with an animal companion's ability to see through our many disguises, discerning who we really are, and still managing an enthusiastic tail wag.

There is another part to the story that is important to mention. It has to do with Joseph Campbell's hero's journey theory. Odysseus is fundamentally changed by his trip. After Argos dies Odysseus says to the herder standing with him:

This is the dog of a man who died far away.

If he were now what he used to be when Odysseus

left and sailed off to Troy, you would be astonished

at his power and speed. No animal could escape him

in the deep forest once he began to track it.

What an amazing nose he had! But misfortune

has fallen upon him now that his master is dead

in some far-distant land,…

As Joseph Campbell puts it regarding the hero's journey it is as if there is a "death of the old…and a resurrection of the new". Odysseus left on his initial journey from home, already known as a charismatic hero but underdeveloped in many other ways. He is unsure of his motives and lacks humility. On one adventure, Odysseus cannot help but claim bragging rights for his ingenious ploy that gets him and his men away from the cave of the one-eyed Cyclops. Bursting with pride that his scheme worked, he reveals his name to the now blinded Cyclops. The fatal mistake sets the stage for the Cyclops' father to get involved. As retribution, Poseidon the god of the sea brings his wrath down on Odysseus and his crew.

After many years of struggle, Odysseus comes to the pivotal moment at the end of the story mentioned above, one that is assisted by his dog Argos. Odysseus has gone through a series of trials and tribulations over the twenty years he has been away. His old nature is swept away, the new aspects take hold. He is older, humbler, and perhaps a bit wiser. As he returns to Ithaca it is not as a proud king with the usual pomp and circumstance befitting a returning hero. Instead, he has been shipwrecked and broken, and his crew lost. He is washed ashore naked on the beach. Putting on the clothing of a beggar not a king, he stands ready to enter the last stage of his quest.

Odysseus, like Argos, has suffered much. Both are alone and in the final stretch of the journey home. With the help of Argos, Odysseus enters his own personal labyrinth, allowing him to feel the heaviness and grief of the previous twenty years. He is not a one-dimensional cut out like so many heroes in stories that came before and after. Instead, he is "the man of twists and turns." Through hard won complexity Odysseus becomes the first "modern man." But he does not do it alone. It is the presence of his loyal canine companion still holding true to his master's memory that offers the needed inspiration to finish what he has started. Argos initiates Odysseus into the brotherhood of the bond.

Epilogue

We see from having explored the various stories in this book, that there is not one specific pattern of the way men and their dogs connect. It occurs sometimes when marriages fail, and careers fade. Other times, there are joint adventures shared in a way that enhances both parties. Sometimes the connection becomes the source of inspiration pushing men further within an inhospitality outer world or even deeper inside the rough terrain of an inner one. Having ventured into various men's life stories, some that may resonate with our own, consider yourself an initiate within the brotherhood of the bond. Whichever category your story falls into: *Artists & Thinkers; Underdog; Healer; Adventurer,* or some mix of each, share your story with others. By doing so, your tale becomes added to the long list of those that went before.

References

1.   Introduction
Levinson, B M (1969). Pet-oriented child psychotherapy. Springfield, Illinois:
Charles C Thomas.

Molnar, M (1996). Of dogs and doggerel. American Imago, 53, (3), 269-280.

Roth, B (2005). Pets and psychoanalysis   A clinical contribution. Psychoanalytic Review, 92, 453-457.

Levinson, B M (1969). Pet-oriented child psychotherapy. Springfield, Illinois:
Charles C Thomas.

2.   When Man meets dog
Blazina,C. When man meets dog. (2016). England, Hubble & Hatie.

Blazina, C, & Bartone, A (2016). Roles of Man's Best Friend in men's lives: Examining the Psychometric Properties of a Measure Assessing Males' HumanAnimal Interactions. In C Blazina & L Kogan (Eds), Men and Their Dogs: A New Understanding of 'Man's Best Friend.' New York: Springer.

Bartone, A, & Blazina, C (2016). Exploring how the human-animal bond affects men in a relational way: Attachment, loss, and gender role conflict in middleaged and young–men. In C Blazina & L Kogan (Eds), Men and Their Dogs: A New Understanding of 'Man's Best Friend.' New York: Springer.

Blazina, C, Boyraz, G, & Shen-Miller, D (Eds). The Psychology of the Human-Animal Bond (pp 203-224). New York: Springer Publishing.

Blazina, C & Kogan, L (2016). Men and Their Dogs: A New Understanding of 'Man's Best Friend. New York: Springer.

3.   Section I Artists & Thinkers

Derr, M. (2004). A Dog's History of America: How Our Best Friend Explored, Conquered, and Settled a Continent. New York: North Point Press.

Gray, B. (2014). The Dog in the Dickensian Imagination. Surrey, Ashgate Publishing.

Howell, P. (2015). At Home and Astray: The Domestic Dog in Victorian Britain. University of Virginia Press.

Strange, JM., Worboys, M., & Pemberton, N. (2018). The Invention of the Modern Dog: Breed and Blood in Victorian Britain. Baltimore: Johns Hopkins Press.

Ritvo, H. (1988). Animal Estate: The English and Other Creatures in the Victorian Age. Cambridge: Harvard.

Wilson. E.O. Biophilia. The Diversity of Life. Library of America.

4.   Home

Gray, B. (2014). The Dog in the Dickensian Imagination. Surrey, Ashgate Publishing.

Kaplan, F. (2013). Dickens: A Biography. Open Road Media.

Slater, M. (2017). Dickens and Women. Edward Everett Root.

Tomalin, C. (2011). Charles Dickens: A Life Hardcover. New York: Penguin Press.

5.   Little dog boy

Stephens, F.G. (2018). Sir Edwin Landseer. Franklin Classics.

6.   Fidelity

Hutchinson, Roger (2005). The soap man : Lewis, Harris and Lord Leverhulme. Edinburgh: Birlinn.

Williams, Olivia (13 October 2019). "The story of Port Sunlight's 'soap king' and his model village". Liverpool Echo.

7.   My fellow sufferer

Cartwright, D.E. (2010). Schopenhauer: A Biography. Cambridge University Press.

8.   A Difference of Degree and Not Kind

Bowlby, J. (1990). Charles Darwin: A New Biography. New York: W.W. Norton.

Darwin, C. (2003). The Origin of Species: 150th Anniversary Edition Mass Market, Signet.

Darwin, C. (2019). The Descent of Man. Digireads.com Publishing.
Darwin, C. (2009). The Expression of the Emotions in Man and Animals, Anniversary Edition 4th Edition. Oxford University Press.

9.   The first friend

Kipling, R. (2011). Thy Servant a Dog and Other Dog Stories. Benediction Classics.

Kipling, R. (2010). The cat that walks by himself. And Other Stories. British Library.

Kipling, R. (1990). Something of Myself and Other Autobiographical Writings. Cambridge University Press.
Montefiore, J. (2007). Rudyard Kipling (Writers and their Work). Northcote House Publishers.

10.   Section II: Underdogs
Blazina, C & Kogan, L (2016). Men and Their Dogs: A New Understanding of 'Man's Best Friend. New York: Springer.
Vandello, J.A., Goldschmied, N., Richards, D.A. R. January (2008), The Appeal of the Underdog, Personality and Social Psychology Bulletin 33(12):1603-16.

11.   The one absolutely unselfish friend
Morrow, L.B. (2012). The Giant Book of Dog Names. Gallery Books.

12.   The Runt

Brooks, Chris. (1989). Burying Tom Sayers. Annual of The Victorian Society.

Chisholm, Hugh, ed. (1911). "Sayers, Tom" . Encyclopædia Britannica. 24 (11th ed.). Cambridge University Press. p. 277.

Wright, Alan. (1994). Tom Sayers: the last great bare-knuckle champion. The Book Guild.

13.   His Master's Voice

"The Nipper Saga". Archived from the original on 24 September 2015.

14.   Prince Hal
Ridley, Jane Bertie, (2008). Bertie : A Life of Edward VII (2008). New York: Penguin Random House.

15.   The little corporal & the grief of one dog

Ellis, G. Napoleon (2016). (Profiles In Power). New York: Routledge.

Roberts, A. (2014)   Napoleon: A Life. New York: Viking.

Tsouras, P.G. (1992). Warrior's words: A quotation book. London, Arms and Armor Press.

16.   Wines, J.A. (2014). Dogs' Miscellany: Everything You Always Wanted to Know About Man's Best Friend. London: Michael O'Mara Books.

17.   Travels with Charley

Steinbeck, J. (1962). Travels with Charley: In Search of America. New York: Penguin.

18.   Section III: Healers

Freud, S (1960). The letters of Sigmund Freud (J S Stern, T, trans). New York: Basic Books.

Levinson, B M (1969). Pet-oriented child psychotherapy. Springfield, Illinois:
Charles C Thomas.

Molnar, M (1996). Of dogs and doggerel. American Imago, 53, (3), 269-280. 9

Roth, B (2005). Pets and psychoanalysis. A clinical contribution. Psychoanalytic Review, 92, 453-457.

19.   St Roch

Aberth, J. (2016). The Black Death, 1348-1350 The Great Mortality of 1348-1350; a Brief History with Documents. Palgrave Macmillan.

20.   His damn dog

Freud, S (1960). The letters of Sigmund Freud (J S Stern, T, trans). New York: Basic Books.
Molnar, M (1996). Of dogs and doggerel. American Imago, 53, (3), 269-

280. 9

Roth, B (2005). Pets and psychoanalysis   A clinical contribution. Psychoanalytic Review, 92, 453-457.

21.   Animal assisted therapy
Levinson, B M (1969). Pet-oriented child psychotherapy. Springfield, Illinois:
Charles C Thomas.

22.   Section IV: Adventurers
Campbell, J. (1973). The Hero With A Thousand Faces. Princeton University Press.

23.   Horatio & Bud
Duncan, Dayton & Burns, Ken (2003). Horatio's Drive: America's First Road Trip (1st ed.). New York: Alfred A. Knopf.

24.   The last explorer
Rose, L.A. (2008). Explorer: The Life of Richard E. Byrd. University of Missouri Press.

25.   I dream of that dog yet

Bragg, Jeffrey (2005). Arthur T. Walden, Dog Driver from the Klondike to Antarctica.

Heald, Bruce D. (2011). A History of Dog Sledding in New England. Charleston: The History Press. pp. 78–80.

26.   The first modern man

Campbell, J. (1973). The Hero With A Thousand Faces. Princeton University Press.

Homer. The Odyssey.

Made in United States
Orlando, FL
13 November 2021